# We Children of Wales

snapshots
of our
lives

Editor:
**Ann Saer**

*"If I climb up to our treehouse, I can see for miles across our fields . . ."* Rhys

*"Going to Nain's is my best thing of all . . ."*

Llinos

Published in 2006 by Pont Books, an imprint of
Gomer Press, Llandysul, Ceredigion SA44 4JL

ISBN 1 84323 426 2
ISBN-13 9781843234265

A CIP record for this title is available from the British Library.

© Pont Books, Gomer Press, 2006

Sponsored by the Welsh Assembly Government

Printed and bound in Wales at
Gomer Press, Llandysul, Ceredigion

2

# Welcome

*"I'm a happy-go-lucky sort of person, really. Maybe I do talk too much at school sometimes . . ."* Arfon

What do children like doing best? Where are their favourite places in Wales? What names do they give their pets? Do they have dreams for the future? How do they feel about school? Which are their favourite foods? What do they have to say about their families?

If you read this book, you'll know the answers to these questions. You'll also get to know a whole bunch of children who have been more than ready to speak for themselves and share their very full and active lives.

We couldn't possibly have included everything the children of Wales know something about - from karate to oyster-farming, braille to poetry, bird-life to quad-bikes. Their knowledge is astonishing. We could never hope to pass on the expertise of 25 children, but what we were able to do was give you snippets of information and mention just some of the books, websites and sources of information that many of the children use at home or in school. Check out what YOU know in these information panels – there's one alongside every child's portrait. You too can become an expert on Wales!

## Did you know?

**● Wales is Wild**
Nearly every child in this book has enjoyed spending time somewhere beautiful – by the sea, in a nature reserve, on a mountain top. They've spotted birds, they've run up mountains, biked around country parks, inspected underwater creatures.

**● History all around you**
Every acre of Wales has a long history – these children know a lot about castles, steam engines, Welsh princes, famous bridges, caves and drovers' roads.

**● Heroes**
Sometimes heroes are great leaders or inventors from the past, sometimes they are sportsmen or women of today and sometimes, according to the children, their grandparents are their real heroes.

**● It's all happening . . .**
From the Urdd Eisteddfod to the Ice Hockey Championships, from the Guto Nyth Brân race to the Royal Welsh Show, children seem to have no trouble deciding 'What's On' – it's a wonder they're ever at home.

# Contents

There are twenty-four portraits in this book – but YOU could make that twenty-five. Turn to page 54 and have a go at designing a new entry, using information you have put together yourself, and pasting in drawings or photographs if you have them. You could do a self-portrait or you could interview someone else – a friend or a family member. And then this book will be even more of a treasure for you to keep. Good luck with the writing and design!

For a colour copy of the pages to work on, you can download pages 54-55 of this book from the website – www.gomer.co.uk (click on Teachersí Resources!)

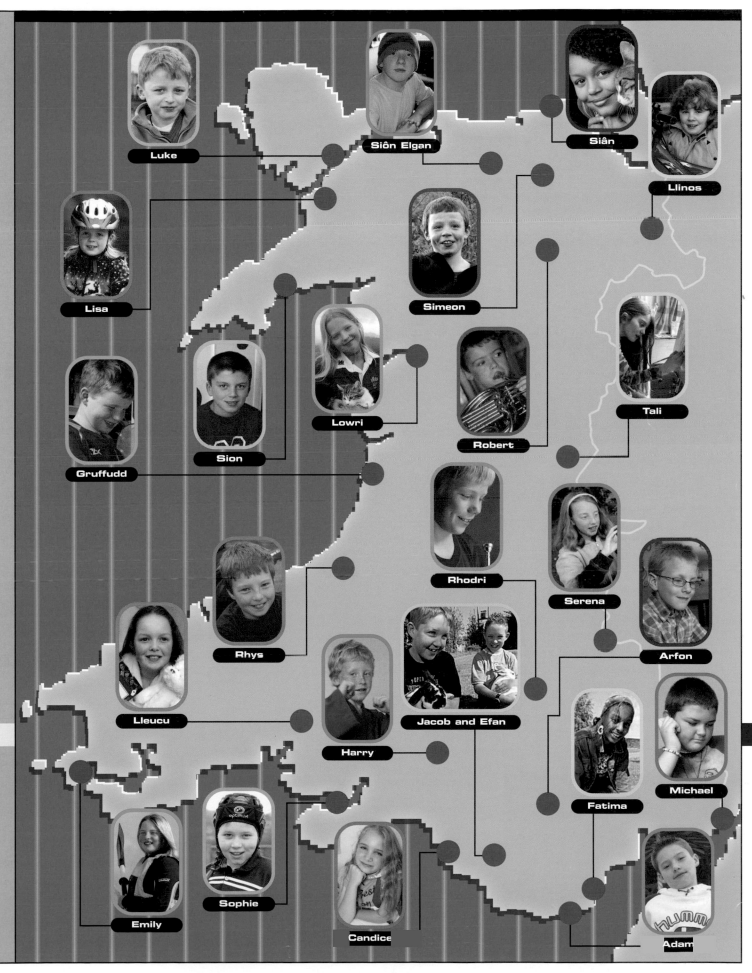

# Rhodri

| | |
|---|---|
| **age** | 10 |
| **birthday** | December |
| **home** | a farmhouse on the Epynt range |
| **family** | parents, brother, 13, and 2 sisters aged 7 and 4 |
| **interests** | cricket, rugby and sports, the trumpet and playing on the farm |

*"I'm really happy being around the farm. What I don't like is going back to school at the end of the holidays."*

Rhodri

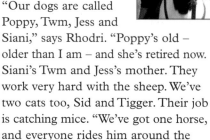

## Farm and family

The old farmhouse where Rhodri and his family live nestles on the slopes of Mynydd Epynt in mid Wales. Years ago, his great-grandfather owned the farm, and Rhodri's grandmother still lives locally. His mother comes from Malvern in Worcestershire. She is now learning Welsh, and all four children speak Welsh and go to a Welsh school. Sometimes Rhodri goes to Malvern to see his grandparents. "We take some of the sheep up in the spring to graze in Granny and Grandad's field, because the grass grows earlier there than it does here. We borrow a trailer from the farm down the road. Everybody helps one another up this way."

## Organic farming

Rhodri's parents met at Reading University when they were both studying agriculture. Now his father works for the Welsh Assembly Government, a job linked to food production, and he helps on the farm at the weekend. Rhodri's mother helps in school as well as looking after the family and working on the farm. And when it's lambing time, the whole family helps. "This is an organic farm. We don't use any chemicals to destroy pests or improve the soil," explains Rhodri. "Mum does the garden and grows veggies like potatoes and carrots. I don't like gardening. Sometimes the sheep get in and gobble up the kidney beans, and Mum goes mad."

## Carnival of animals

In the morning, Rhodri often wakes up to a cacophony of competing animal voices. Welsh Black cattle in the nearby cowshed low loudly for their breakfast. In the fields, more than a hundred Speckled-faced Beulah sheep enjoy an early morning bleat. Though there are no ducks to quack, the hens cackle and quarrel, and the dogs bark excitedly. "Our dogs are called Poppy, Twm, Jess and Siani," says Rhodri. "Poppy's old – older than I am – and she's retired now. Siani's Twm and Jess's mother. They work very hard with the sheep. We've two cats too, Sid and Tigger. Their job is catching mice. "We've got one horse, and everyone rides him around the farm. Well, all except Dad, who's tall, and the horse is a bit short."

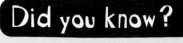

## At school

Rhodri, Gareth, Delyth and Megan travel on the school bus every morning along narrow, twisting country lanes. It's quite an adventure, especially in winter. Sometimes when the weather's really bad, the bus can't reach them.

"When there's snow, we can go sledging on the steep slope above the farm," says Rhodri. "That's one of my best things. Nearly as good as the first day of the holidays!

It's not that I don't like school, though. I enjoy Welsh and maths and PE, especially rugby and cricket. And the Eisteddfod. I was in the recitation group that went to the Urdd Eisteddfod in Cardiff. And I like it when a speaker comes in to school. Penri Roberts came in to help us to write a poem in Welsh, and Jenny Sullivan came to help us with a story based on a picture of a flying dragon and a man in armour. I prefer listening to people, rather than talking all the time myself."

### ✔ Cricket, football – and the trumpet

Rhodri is a great fan of cricket. When England and Australia were playing for the Ashes, he was glued to the television set. He's been down to the Sophia Gardens cricket ground in Cardiff, too to watch a game. "I'm thrilled to bits when I get picked for trials," says Rhodri. By now, he plays for Brecon as well as once a fortnight for mid-Wales, travelling to places like Llandrindod. "Chicken curry and Mum's Sunday dinner keep me going, though Mum says I should eat more veggies."

Playing the trumpet is a good exercise for the lungs, too. And as for football, Rhodri's favourite team is Aston Villa.

### ✔ Fun with friends

Friends mean a lot to Rhodri. Though his home is isolated, there's always a buzz there. Nearly every weekend and holiday, friends come to play with Rhodri and his brother Gareth. The trampoline's very popular with them all.

"I've got five special friends," explains Rhodri. "When they're here, we often play up the top, near the mountain, building cities out of stones. Or we play card games like 'Spit' with Gareth and Delyth. Megan's still a bit too young yet."

## Did you know?

- that 'Epynt' means 'the way of the horses'?

- that 'Malvern' comes from two old Welsh words, 'moel fryn'- bleak hill?

- that long, long ago, Old Welsh used to be spoken in the counties on the English side of the Welsh border? Welsh place-names there became anglicised. Perhaps you can think of other place-names which show the effect of bilingualism.

- that the first Welsh banks were set up because of the Welsh Black cattle? Cattle and sheep used to be 'exported' to English fairs by the drovers. On their way home, highwaymen would often lie in wait to steal the money the drovers carried after selling the animals. In the end, David Jones, one of the drovers, set up a bank in Llandovery where the money could be kept safely. It was called 'The Bank of the Black Ox'. The building is now home to a HSBC bank.

- that if you love getting muddy, the annual Bog Snorkelling Contest in the small spa town of Llanwrtyd could be just the place for you? In the past, people who were ill used to go there to bathe and drink water from the local wells, hoping to be cured. Now they go there to have fun in the peaty mud of Mynydd Epynt.

### ✔ Concerts and barbecues

Near Rhodri's home, an old school has been turned into a community centre. Harvest suppers and Christmas concerts are held there, while barbecues and sports are held in an adjoining field. Rhodri's family and friends and neighbours all go and have a good time together.

"It's almost as good as our camping holidays in Pembrokeshire. I'm allowed to bring a friend and we go to the beach every day to swim and build dams and look for sandworms – the ones that puffins eat – and crabs. Really great!"

# Lisa

| age | 8 |
|---|---|
| birthday | June |
| home | red-brick house in a village near Caernarfon |
| family | parents and sister, 5 |
| interests | cycling, gymnastics, ballet and travelling |

## Mam and Dad and Nia

Lisa's mother is from just up the road in the village, but her father is from Brisbane, Australia – the other side of the world! Lisa's mother was a teacher before she gave up work to look after the girls. Her father is a doctor whose first language is English, though he has learned to speak Welsh by now. But Lisa speaks English to him sometimes. "I just like the language," she says.

But Lisa and Nia always speak Welsh to each other. The two sisters are great friends and choose to share a bedroom even though the house has a spare room. Sometimes they chat (quietly) for a long time before going to sleep.

"When there's no school, I go to bed at 10 o'clock, but if there's school, I go at half-past-seven."

## Nain and Grandpa

"Nain lives a quarter-of-a-mile up the road and she's made part of her house into a café which has the best cakes in Wales. I see her nearly every day and in the holidays I help in the café. I love having Nain living so close."

### A family trip along Lôn Eifion

Sometimes at the week-end, the family go cycling on the special bike-track which runs nearby – Lôn Eifion.

"I go on the cycle-track all the way from here to Pen-y-groes with Mam and Dad and Nia – everyone but Dad has a bike. He has to run after us. Sometimes Nia goes too fast and, once she's started, she can't stop. If Dad wasn't able to catch her in time, maybe she'd reach Australia!"

"*There's something very special about a sleepover at Nain's.*"

Lisa's grandfather lives much further away, in Australia. Lisa remembers going there to see him. "One morning, we went to this café – there was no time for me to change, and I had to go in my pyjamas!" Grandpa is a bit of a character. Though he's just had his seventieth birthday, he still cycles a lot. And one of the high points of Lisa's week is on Sunday morning, when she and Nia use a computer and the internet to talk to Grandpa as well as see him on the monitor screen.

Though Grandpa comes over to Wales to see her nearly every year, Lisa misses him a lot. "I'd like to go and live in Australia, but then I'd miss Nain terribly."

## Travelling the world

As well as Australia, Lisa has been all the way to:

✔ **the USA** when she flew over Niagara Falls in a helicopter

✔ **Legoland in Denmark** where even the chips in the café were Lego-shaped!

✔ **Lapland** where she met Santa Claus, in a little wooden hut in a forest, miles from anywhere. "He didn't speak Welsh but I had gel pens and Angelina Ballerina and a backpack to keep clothes and ballet shoes. I gave Santa Claus a present, too – a little book about Wales just to make sure he knows where to bring presents for Nia and myself at Christmas."

## School

Painting and crafts are Lisa's favourite activities. "We've been making a castle out of cardboard, with lollipop sticks for the people, and there's a door you can open with a cord."

Lisa likes singing in the morning assembly, too. And once she played the piano in front of all the other children.

## Sports and ballet lessons

Tuesdays are for swimming! Lisa swims at school during the day and again in the evening with Hans the instructor, who is strict and makes them work hard. Lisa has swum the width of the pool about twenty times and the length about four times. "I stop and hold on to the side every time, though. I can do the front crawl, breaststroke and backstroke. Once a week, I have a tennis lesson with Andreas who's German and a real 'case'."

## Saturdays

"I have a ballet lesson with Miss Tami in Pwllheli in the morning – about half-an-hour away by car. Boys used to come, but only girls come now."

On Saturdays, Lisa also has gymnastics lessons. It was there that she learned the skills that she had to perform accurately to win a medal.

"I had to jump on a springboard and off the box, then do a stretch jump and land neatly with my feet on the floor, then do a roly-poly, a half-turn and a backwards roll. I didn't expect to win at all – we'd already left the leisure centre, and Dad's mobile went off in the car to say I'd won and we had to go back all the way to collect the medal. It was a really nice surprise!"

## Did you know?

• It would have taken Lisa months to have reached Australia 150 years ago. She would have had to travel – perhaps from Porthmadog or very probably from Liverpool – in a sailing ship, which depended on the wind for its speed. She would have sailed down south, past South Africa and the Cape of Good Hope, over the Indian Ocean to Australia. Then she'd have crossed the Pacific Ocean and down past South America, rounding Cape Horn before crossing the Atlantic back to the Irish Sea and home to Wales. Hasta la Vista, Lisa! See you in about a year's time, perhaps?

• If Lisa had travelled in 1881 on a big steam-driven liner, she'd have been able to get there in 42 days – say a month-and-a-half. She could have shortened her journey by going through the Bay of Biscay and the Mediterranean Sea, and cut through the Suez Canal into the Red Sea and then into the Indian Ocean.

• By today, Lisa can get to Australia in less than 24 hours! For more information about ships and the sea, look up www.museumwales.ac.uk/en/swansea

# Siôn Elgan

| age | 10 |
|---|---|
| birthday | October |
| home | a country village in Denbighshire |
| family | parents, sisters 15 and 6, and brother, 12 |
| interests | rugby, golf and playing with friends |

*"Sometimes in my upper bunk before going to sleep I think about things, like the worst thing that ever happened to me – the time I was knocked off my bike by a car, though I didn't break anything. Or the best thing, which was coming second in a belching competition in Y Bala. Or I have a look at my Real Madrid Poster, and dream I'm Robinhio, or Superman. And then I go to sleep."*

Siôn

## Siôn Elgan's family – and his friends

Siôn and his family live in a manse because his father's a minister. His mother is a supply teacher. Siôn says his family are always very busy, but that sometimes they spend a day out cycling or walking around Llyn Brenig, a reservoir not far away which has lots of leisure facilities.

Usually, Siôn gets on well with his sisters and brother. "Sometimes, though, Catrin (who's brainy) and Steffan (who's a very good rugby player) can be annoying. But Hanna's okay. In fact, I'm quite glad to have a younger sister, because before she was born Steffan used to tease me about being the youngest. He doesn't any more because Hanna's the baby now."

Siôn's two best friends live nearby, one of them just four houses away. "If I shout at the top of my voice out in the garden, he can hear me!" says Siôn.

## Golf

Although Siôn used to like football and rollerblading, he now enjoys golf best of all. Sometimes he and his father go to the driving range in St Asaph, but usually they practise in the field by the manse.

"One day I hit the ball through one of the chapel windows and smashed it. That was a bit embarrassing for both of us."

## Fashion

Siôn likes to wear a 'hoodie' and baggy jeans. "A 'hoodie' is a top with a hood and it's all the better if there are little holes at the end of the sleeves so that you can stick your thumbs out and look really cool," explains Siôn. "And if we want something special, we shop in Llandudno or Chester."

## A typical day in Siôn's life, in his own words

### Before school

"I wake at 7.15, before Steffan, who sleeps in the lower bunk. I jump down and draw the curtains, and this is what I see:

**1** Tryfan, our golden retriever, scampering round the yard. My dad, who likes climbing, named him after his favourite mountain.

**2** the fields belonging to Hendre Llan Farm and Nant y Plwm Woods. One steep field is especially good for sledging. Snow falls here most years, and last winter we made a ramp out of an old door. It was like a ski-jump in the Olympics!

**3** the graveyard and chapel where my dad's the minister. If he's late for a service, I can see him taking a short cut over the garden wall, running across the field and leaping over the graveyard wall to get into the pulpit in time. I go to Sunday School and try to be a really good boy because Mam's my teacher. She's okay, because she lets us play pool for a little while before the lesson. My favourite Bible story's the one about Noah's Ark. It reminds me of the floods in 2001, when the road was like a river, and the school was closed for the day – great!

**4** the posts in the Community Centre's football field. Everything happens in the Community Centre – eisteddfodau, meetings, weddings, funeral teas, plays and concerts. That's where my school is, too.

After breakfast, I rush to school so that we can play football for a while before the bell. I play in the school team and I'm the one who takes the penalties. I try to keep the ball down low and kick it hard into the corner. I don't often miss, and I have never been sent off the field, though I did have a warning once.

### In school

If the first lesson's PE, I'm happy, but I really don't like maths. The only thing that makes me feel worse than a maths lesson is when it rains at playtime and we can't go out in the yard. I don't like speaking English in the yard. Most of us are from Welsh-speaking homes. Mam speaks English sometimes, because it's her first language. But she's learned Welsh well and that's what she usually speaks. And though both Mam and Dad come from south Wales, I know I'm a *gog* and not a *hwntw* because I speak north Wales Welsh. I say *i fyny* and Dad says *lan*, (for the word 'up'), and I say *rwan* and Dad says *nawr*, (for the word 'now').

All morning, I look forward to dinner-time. I like school dinners. The roast potatoes are even better than Mam's. I'd prefer Macdonald's, though.

### After school

When the bell rings at the end of the afternoon, I rush out to buy sweets at the village shop before going home. One night a week I go to the children's club in chapel, where we sing, learn about Jesus and play games. Afterwards, as usual, I'll play football again, or go down to the river to play Tarzan, swinging on a rope, and sometimes I fall in…"

## Did you know?

● that Llyn Brenig is one of the biggest reservoirs in Wales? You can walk, fish and take part in water sports on this lake, set in the heathery Denbighshire moors. Celtic, Roman and Norman warriors once marched across here. Now, sheep have taken over. Llyn Brenig is looked after by a company called Welsh Water, which makes sure you have clean drinking water. It also gets rid of the water you use when you shower, clean your teeth and flush the toilet.

● that in the area where Siôn Elgan lives young people often do really well and become famous? The young singer, dancer and actress Tara Bethan and the author Gwenno Mair Davies who won the Urdd Eisteddfod crown were both brought up here. The artist and sculptor Luned Rhys Parry is also from the area. She helped pupils from the school create a collage of the village, and one of her collages hangs on a wall in Siôn's home. Another celebrity is Tudur Aled, a poet who lived there 500 years ago. He was as famous in Wales then as any of today's sporting heroes and pop stars are now. And William Salesbury and Bishop William Morgan, translators of the Bible into Welsh are other famous people from this part of Wales.

# Candice

*"I do a lot of things at school, like cycling and netball. We go swimming to Aberavon as well, and I really like that."*

| age | 10 |
|---|---|
| birthday | February |
| home | a house near Port Talbot |
| family | her mum, dad and Heskey the dog |
| interests | dancing, boy band 'Busted', swimming and netball |

Candice is the kind of girl who likes to join in everything.

## The Dance Club

"I've just joined. It's a new club for girls and boys. We do disco-dance routines which are good exercise and fun. We get sheets of paper with the routines on them, so that we can practise at home. We raised some money for Children in Need by performing a routine and holding a raffle."

## Music, bands and acting

Candice plays 'Titanic' with a recorder group in school assemblies, which she really enjoys. But she is happiest listening to her favourite bands, such as Busted.

"I love it when they are on TV, and I'm looking forward to seeing their new show, 'America or Busted'. I went down to see them in Singleton Park in Swansea, and I got autographs from the other bands playing as well. I've got loads of photographs of Busted."

Candice likes being on stage herself. She has always been in the school Nativity play, and this year she landed the role of Mary. "I was chosen out of about fifteen girls in all, so I was really pleased about that."

## And how about school?

Candice enjoys history and maths best at school. In science, her class is studying the solar system. "I'm making a model of the solar system at home and I've been collecting various bits and bobs to make it. I always like making stuff."

## Did you know?

- that one of the top ten places in the world to ride a mountain bike is in the Afan Argoed Forest Park in the Afan valley, not far from Candice's home? It has over 100 kilometres of cycle track, and you can walk and horse-ride there too. It's run by the Forestry Commission.

- that though it looks so industrialised, with its dramatic steelworks, Port Talbot has a nature reserve with one of the largest badger setts in Wales, and you can see red deer and lots of other wildlife at nearby Margam Park – as well as some spooky abbey ruins?

You won't find any oranges in the Orangery any more, though maybe there'll be a few ghostly monks around.

- that Richard Burton and Anthony Hopkins, two of the world's most famous actors, both came from the Port Talbot area, as well as Michael Sheen, whose star is still rising?

Sounds a good place for a day out? Look up Neath/Port Talbot on the internet to find out more, and try htttp://homepage.ntlworld.com/badger10 for badger news.

The school has a points system, and Candice tries her best to win points for her house. "You get five points for doing your homework and you can gain extra points if you're good, for example, if you find money that's not yours and you give it to the teacher."

She's also a keen member of the Library Club in school: "We read books and then we write about them or go on the internet to find interesting things about them. It's a way of getting other children to come to the library, and it's worked, too. A poetry book called *Star in the Custard* was launched in the library and I found that really good."

Candice's favourite book is *Charlie and the Chocolate Factory* but she's also read three of the Harry Potter books. "And I love books about history. At the moment we're doing the Tudors, so I'm reading books and finding things on the internet about them."

## Favourite Animals

Candice is an only child and Heskey the dog keeps her company. He's really friendly. "Daddy called him Heskey after the football player, because he loves playing football. Every time I play with the ball, he takes the ball off me. He's so funny!"

✔ **She loves taking Heskey for a walk.**

"The beach isn't far, and he likes going down there for a walk. I get a chance then to collect shells and look for crabs and things in the rock pools. We're really lucky to have the beach; it's somewhere to go and chill out in summer."

✔ **Dolphins**

Candice loves dolphins and she gets angry when she hears about them being killed. "Norway and Japan say they're doing it for scientific reasons. In America as well, lots of dolphins are killed in nets put up to stop sharks, but the poor dolphins get stuck in them and drown. I keep on asking Daddy if I can adopt a dolphin."

## Family

Candice's father is an environmental engineer. He works for a dismantling company employed by the Port Talbot steelworks. "He deals with waste products and hazardous substances like asbestos. He's got a very impressive mask that's a bit frightening, really!"

Candice's mother is a housewife, and also helps out with the family. "My grandfather hasn't been well, so Mum takes turns with my other aunts and uncles to look after him. My cousin and I help too. We hope he'll be better soon."

## And what are Candice's hopes for the future?

"I'd like to learn the guitar and perhaps be in a band. And I wouldn't mind getting good grades when I go to the comprehensive school. Inventing something new wouldn't be bad either . . . and I've been asking Daddy if he can save up so that I can have a horse, but he says that's 'wishful thinking'."

Whatever happens, you can be sure that Candice will join in everything she can!

# Rhys

| | |
|---|---|
| **age** | 9 |
| **birthday** | May |
| **home** | a farm in the Aberaeron area, Ceredigion |
| **family** | parents and two brothers, 11 and 9 |
| **interests** | acting and reciting, quad biking, swimming, reading, cooking and Xbox games |

*Rhys*

> **"***I like living in the country. I've travelled to lots of other places like London and Florida, but I prefer the countryside. I like seeing fields and trees. If I climb up to our treehouse, I can see for miles across our fields, to fields which belong to other farms.***"**

## Rhys's family

Rhys's father was brought up in London, where his family used to sell milk. "But even there, he spoke Welsh, because he went to the London Welsh School. He came back to the Aberaeron area when he was 11. Sometimes I help Dad on the farm with the sheep.

Dan the sheepdog helps as well. I open and shut the gates and walk behind the sheep with Dad, and help him with the big bales."

Rhys's mother used to be a cook before she got married. "She's a very good cook. I'm allowed to cook too, and I like making chocolate cornflake cakes. Mam's the one who takes us to school every day. I usually like school, especially playtime, when I run around with my friend, Dafydd. On Sundays I go to Sunday school, and I learn a verse to say."

Rhys has two brothers, Aled and Tudur. "Aled is the eldest and Tudur is the youngest, so I'm the one in the middle," says Rhys. "Sometimes we fight if we want to play with the same thing, but usually we're good friends. Aled has extra help in school. A few years ago, he was really ill with leukaemia, and he had to go to hospital very often. But he's fine now."

## Rhys's favourite things

"I enjoy the same kinds of things as other children," says Rhys. "Here are some of them:

✔ reading (Dick King-Smith's books)
✔ drawing
✔ quad biking
✔ Xbox games and the computer
✔ swimming in the pool in Aberaeron

When it's fine in summer, though, it's better swimming in the sea. Beaches like New Quay and Cei Bach aren't far away. But my favourite thing of all, I think, is the quad bike. I had it as a Christmas present last year. It's an 80cc Yamaha. I enjoy speeding around the fields. My brothers each have a quad bike too, but we're not allowed to race each other. We wear our everyday clothes and a helmet to keep us safe."

## Drama and reciting

Rhys enjoys reciting and is a member of a drama society in Aberaeron. "We performed *Aye Aye, Captain* in Theatr Felinfach," says Rhys. "I've been to see several London shows too, like *The Lion King* and *Chitty-Chitty-Bang-Bang!* Once, when I broke my arm, Mam said I'd have to go to the theatre. I thought, hooray! I'm on my way to see a show. And then I realised I was going to the theatre in the hospital to have surgery!

I've been reciting in an eisteddfod recently. The piece I recited was by a Welsh poet called T. Llew Jones. It's about a highwayman, and is very dramatic."

## An unforgettable experience

"One of the best experiences I've ever had was going to the Urdd Eisteddfod in Anglesey to compete in the action song. I had the main part – a mouse. We had to sing and act. We practised for months, and after winning in the local and county eisteddfodau, we were tremendously excited. The whole family went up to stay in Llandudno. There were so many lights and cameras, I felt really nervous in the beginning about performing on stage. But I soon got used to it, and it's great looking at the video."

## Holidays

Sometimes the family goes on holiday in their caravan to stay at the Royal Welsh Show and the National Eisteddfod. "The Royal Welsh is interesting because of all the animals and machines. This year, I showed a lamb there. I had to wear a white coat, and walk around the ring with the lamb on a lead. In future, I'd like to show more animals, and join the Young Farmers' Club when I'm old enough."

The family has been to Florida to the seaside and to visit Disneyland. "The best bit was swimming with the dolphins and visiting Universal Studios, especially the 3D Shrek. That was really, truly something I'll never forget."

# Fatima

Fatima and her family came to Cardiff from the Sudan nearly two years ago and now she speaks English as well as she speaks Arabic. They live in quite a small flat, which is a new experience for Fatima.

| age | 11 |
| --- | --- |
| birthday | November |
| home | A flat near Cardiff Bay |
| family | Her mother and two sisters, 8 (who is a good artist) and 4 (a real chatterbox) |
| interests | Dancing, rap, acting, reading, writing and lots of other activities |

"In Sudan, we had a very big house with many rooms, and a pear tree and lemon trees in the garden, and many coloured flowers, and a swing. And I used to keep fish, and a boy-budgerigar who was really a hen. We had lots of birds, too – canaries and parrots, but they used to fly away all the time. I really miss them. There isn't room here for pets. I really want a cat or dog – or a snake or a lizard!"

*"If I could, I would like to stop people fighting and stealing. When I grow up, maybe I could travel round the world telling them to stop."*

## What she likes doing...

✔ **painting...**
"I helped students from the Art School to do a huge mural downstairs."

✔ **dancing and gymnastics and rap music...**
"I go to a club which is held for us every night downstairs and we paint and disco-dance and we act and we took part in a concert in the Coal Exchange down in the Bay. And I go swimming every Saturday."

*Fatima*

✔ **writing...**
"I get good marks in school for my long stories. I like to try and make them really thrilling, with gripping beginnings, and I tell about my life here in letters to my friends in the Sudan, and I keep a diary, a secret diary…"

✔ **reading...**
"long books, every night before I go to sleep. I like the author Jacqueline Wilson best, and the 'Famous Five' books. There is a library at school where we can borrow books and I have my own card now for Cardiff Library."

✔ **watching...**
"cartoons and *MTV* and *The Ministry of Mayhem* on television."

✔ **cooking...**
"Sometimes girls don't like it, but I do. I make spaghetti and noodles for us and I like experimenting. My favourite foods are: steak, meatballs, chicken and pizza."

✔ **playing the piano...**
"I play children's songs and Arabic songs and now I have lessons on Saturdays."

✔ **visiting places...**
"like the Brecon Beacons, and Castell Coch, and St. Fagans, and the Gower, where we stayed in a tent and we got soaked!"

## And doesn't like doing...

✘ "I really don't like taking the clothes to be washed. It gets very full in the laundry room so I have to wait and it gets very boring. And I don't like it when my sisters bring their friends home, and they mess up the room with their toys, and they don't tidy it up. And then I do it."

### And how about school?

"I go to an English school in the week, and Arabic school on Sunday. I have Welsh lessons in the English school, and I know who St David was. I like science and history and art and indoor PE though sometimes I get bored. I'm in the school football team, too. I really love dinner-times when I can play with my friends. And we made this garden in the playground, an Islamic garden like a star with eight points made from mosaics, and five trees to show the five pillars of Islam, and a herb garden, and places for people to sit down. There was a picture of us with the garden in the paper because we won this national competition. I was very happy about that.

I am leader of our school council and we sort out fights and stop litter and things like that. The other children voted to put us on the council. I'd like to think I was chosen because I like peace and order. And I like listening to people. I'd prefer to think I was chosen for my personality, not because I was somebody's friend."

### Did you know?

• that one of the most exciting buildings in the world stands on the waterfront in Cardiff Bay? It's the Cardiff Millennium Centre, built from Welsh stone, slate, glass and steel, and mighty enough to stand up to the power of the wind and weather. If you come to it from the west at dusk, the buildings' layers or strata look like great cliffs. And the letter-shaped windows cut high into the great steel roof shimmer like jewels, spelling out words by the poet Gwyneth Lewis: In These Stones Horizons Sing/*Creu Gwir Fel Gwydr O Ffwrnais Awen* (creating truth like glass from inspiration's furnace).

• This centre for opera and musicals, ballet and dance is also the home of Urdd Gobaith Cymru. The Urdd is one of

### Arabic school

"On Sunday, everything is in Arabic. In Arabic school, we learn about religion and read the Qur'an, and in my class we are studying for a GCSE in Arabic. My mother speaks Arabic to us at home though she speaks English very well and has a degree in econometrics and she is still studying. She is afraid we will forget Arabic because we only hear it on Sundays. Sometimes I speak English with Sahar and Leena. But when I write letters to my friends and my grandparents and uncles and aunts who live in the Sudan and Dubai and Sweden and the USA, I always write in Arabic."

Europe's largest youth organisations, founded by Sir Ifan ab Owen Edwards in 1922. Perhaps you've already been to one of its camps to swim, ski, pony-trek or take part in other activities. From now on, you can also stay at the Millennium Centre, taking part in workshops and performances organised by the Urdd, or visit the biggest youth festival in Europe, the Urdd National Eisteddfod, which will be held there every four years. There are more competitors in the Urdd Eisteddfod than even the Olympic Games. Find out more on the Urdd's (very busy) website: www.urdd.org

### Fatima's angry when...

• my sisters don't help.
• people shout at you.
• people leave you out.
• anyone fights my sisters – I'll always go to tell someone.

### When she grows up...

"I'd really like to be a doctor. I have uncles who are doctors. I used to play doctors and patients...diagnosing what's wrong, but I don't like the thought of taking blood."

### What makes her jump for joy?

"Hearing from my family because I am very proud of my grandfather, who is a Federal Supreme Judge, and my grandmother who is a sort of adviser in education, and my uncle who is a professor of neurology, and my aunt who is a professor of pathology and I miss them.

### and

Eid, which is a great celebration for Muslim people like us. It happens after Ramadan, which is a time when people fast. Well, the children don't fast, only the older people. For Eid, we have new clothes and go to the mosque, and have many presents or money and there is no school. We have really special food, too, like Kisra, which is a very thin bread which you eat with a kind of sauce."

### Maybe, one day...

Fatima's dreams will come true and she will live in a really big villa: "I'd have my own bedroom decorated in purple, or cream, or blue, and my own TV and stereo – perhaps in Florida, by Disneyland, or on a Caribbean island, where I could do tropical diving, and a jungle – or perhaps a rainforest. Maybe in Australia?"

# Sion

| | |
|---|---|
| **age** | 9 |
| **birthday** | October |
| **home** | Eifionydd, Gwynedd |
| **family** | his parents, a sister, 7 and a brother, 5 |
| **interests** | dancing, painting, singing, running, and French |

Sion

> **"***I can speak Welsh, English and French, though Welsh is best! My mother is Welsh, but I have a French surname because my dad's French. People who don't know us say 'Herbert', but the right way to say it is 'Eber'.***"**

## Sion and *français*

Sion was born in France, but his family moved to Wales when he was five months old. Now he lives in the countryside in one of the most beautiful and most visited parts of Wales.

"Dad always speaks French to me, and I go to see Mami and Papi (Grandma and Grandpa) in France every year. They live in Paris and La Baule, and I speak only French to them. They call me 'Siyn'. Mam speaks French well too, but I don't speak French to her. It would feel odd."

## French food

"I like France. The beaches are good. Too much salad and tomatoes, though. But the *crêpes* (the chocolate ones and the ones that are set on fire) are nice, and the puddings that Papi makes, things like chocolate mousse. I like the breakfasts there as well, usually a (pink!) bowl of *chocolat*, and a *brioche* (a kind of sweet bread) or a *croissant*, but back home in Wales, I have Weetabix."

## Celine and Dylan

Sion says Celine likes playing school in her bedroom, and writing and illustrating stories. His little brother Dylan likes insects!

## ✔ Dancing

Sion has been having dancing lessons for a year with a company called 'Dance for All', where he learns 'dancing-acting' and mime and different modern dance routines.

"I've always liked dancing and now I practise at home nearly every night. I get really cross when Celine comes in when I'm trying out something I've made up. I like dancing to 'Cha Cha Slide' by DJ Casper, and I like the way Rachel Stevens dances – and the band S Club 8. It'd be good to have a Welsh band like them - maybe me and my friends could start one!"

## ✔Pictures and painting....

Though Sion likes painting, he doesn't want to be an artist when he grows up. He says he'd prefer to work in advertising, because he likes creating pictures. "My bedroom's crammed with all kinds of pictures – I've even painted the wardrobe. My favourite school subjects are technology and art and I love painting, pottery and printing and things like that."

# Sion's French lesson

| hello | Ça va | (sar var) |
|---|---|---|
| good morning | bonjour | (bawnzhoor) |
| please | s'il vous plaît | (see voo pleh) |
| thank you | merci | (merr-see) |
| goodbye/see you soon | au revoir | (aw rrevwah) |
| chips | les frites | (lay freet) |
| crisps | les chips | (lay sheeps) |
| ice cream | une glace | (oon glass) |
| one, two three | un/une*, deux, trois | (ern/oon,der,trwa) |
| apple | une pomme | (oon pom) |
| water | l'eau | (l'oh) |
| I'm hungry | J'ai faim | (shay fam) |
| I'm thirsty | J'ai soif | (shay swav) |
| I'm tired | Je suis fatigué | (sher swee fateegay) |
| I'm Welsh | Je suis Gallois/Galloise* | (sher swee gallwa/gallwas) |
| Wales | Pays de Galles | (pay der gall) |

*depends whether the noun is masculine or feminine (as in Welsh)

## ✔...and reading...

"I don't read that much, but I do enjoy stuff by Jacqueline Wilson and Roald Dahl. I've seen the Harry Potter films – they were cool, and so were *The Cat in the Hat* and *Shrek*. And I quite like writing mystery and adventure stories."

## ✔...and shopping at Ikea

"It's my favourite shop in all the world. Why? Because it's so modern and stylish. I could happily spend a whole day there, and I've got a lamp from Ikea in my bedroom. When I grow up, I shall have a house full of things from Ikea, though I'll probably keep the Bambi picture Papi made for me when I was small, and the sampler made when I was born, and Cara, a dog teddy I had from Santa Claus last Chrismas."

## Tourists

Because thousands of visitors come to Eifionydd every year to enjoy the sea and the mountains, to see the castle at Cricieth and Lloyd George's museum at Llanystumdwy, many of the people who live there all the year round work in the holiday industry. Sion's father is a chef and kept a restaurant for many years, and his mother works in a hotel. The family also rent out holiday cottages.

"Sometimes children come to stay, and we play with them. Usually they're from cities like London and Manchester, and sometimes from Cardiff. They like to see the sheep and lambs in the fields, and going on the see-saw and the swings. They say things like: 'This place is cool!' and 'This place is humungous!' Because where they live, there aren't any farm animals, or woods. I have to say I do like living here, in the middle of nowhere, out in the countryside."

SION MEIRION

# Harry

| age | 8 |
| --- | --- |
| birthday | March |
| home | a terraced house in a village close to the Brecon Beacons National Park |
| family | Mum here in Wales, Dad in London and Gran in Ludlow |
| interests | keeping fit, karate, mountain biking, cars, playing the trumpet and reading |

Harry lives in the very house where his great-grandmother used to live, almost a hundred years ago. From his bedroom window, he looks out over the mountain known as 'The Sleeping Giant' and over on the other side are the Dan yr Ogof caves. "The caves are great fun for children who like finding out about dinosaurs and fossils."

## School

Harry lives close enough to his school to walk there every day. "We do many subjects in English and some in Welsh. Maths is my favourite subject. I'm also good at history and I like working on the computer. But the best part of my day is seeing my friends." Harry has started learning the trumpet at school too, and recently got a silver in the Junior Brass Certificate. Maybe one day he'll play in one of the area's famous silver or brass bands.

## After-school club

After school, Harry goes to an after-school club. "My mum works until half-past-five and can't pick me up from school. We play pool and there's a Playstation. There are mobis – things with two wheels you've got to try and walk on, a DVD and video player. In winter, when it's dark, we can do crafts and I like making paper aeroplanes. It's good fun because you get to meet new friends."

> *"When you've reached the fifth degree black belt, you know it all."*
>
> *Harry*

## Keeping Fit

Keeping fit is very important for Harry. "I like skipping; the other boys think it's a girly thing to do, but it's an excellent way to keep fit." Harry eats health foods as well. His favourite food is a selection of fruit on a plate, and he'd much prefer an apple to a bar of chocolate.

## Karate

Karate also keeps Harry fit. He goes to a karate club twice a week and he's already on his fifth belt: a green belt with a white stripe. "Our instructor is very nice and kind; he doesn't shout at you. There's quite a lot you have to remember with karate. Your hands make fists. One fist goes up by your chin and the other goes out in front in different ways. If you have your left hand in front, you put your left foot forward, and if you have your right hand in front, you put your right foot forward." Harry feels that karate has

helped him a lot: "It's improved my self-defence skills and it's taught me discipline. You learn that you have to keep calm if someone is picking on you," he says. Harry's aim is to become a black belt. "First I've got to get a solid green belt, then I want to move through the other belts: purple, blue, brown and then black."

## Trigger

Harry has a dog called Trigger. "He's two years old, but it seems as if we've had him for years. When he's on his back he likes to have his belly tickled. But if someone annoys him he can growl a bit."

## Indoors

✔When he's at home, Harry enjoys reading. "I like adventure stories and spooky stories."

✔He also plays card games such as 'Pairs' as well as games like 'Spiderman 2' on his Playstation.

✔Harry knows a lot about cars and likes reading car magazines and watching *Top Gear* and *Scrappy Races* where people build cars from pieces of scrap. His favourite car is a McLaren F1. "It has 680 brake horse power and six gears. I like watching the Grand Prix and my favourite driver is Ralf Schumacher because he drives for the McLaren Mercedes team."

## Did you know?

● that if you're an adventurous, outdoorsy person like Harry that the upper Swansea Valley could be just the place for you? It adjoins the stunning Brecon Beacons National Park, one of 24 specially protected European Geoparks. Here you can go pony trekking and mountain biking, cycling and walking, play golf, abseil and climb mountains like Cefn Carn Fadog and Carreg Goch. Or maybe you enjoy canoeing and rafting, or searching out majestic waterfalls. Take care, though: countryside trails can be slippery.

● that if you go to a place called Caerbont near Abercrave and look over to the hill called Y Cribarth, you can see what seems to be the outline of a huge man, lying on his back? Find out more from 'The Sleeping Giant Foundation' on www.sgfnet.co.uk – or maybe you could write your own story about how he came to be sleeping there.

● that if you happen to go picnicking in Craig-y-nos Country Park, not far from Dan yr Ogof, and listen carefully you might just hear the ghostly strains of an Italian opera wafting in from the castle nearby. The world-famous soprano Adelina Patti used to live there a hundred years ago. Rich Madam Patti was as well-known then as Bryn Terfel and Katherine Jenkins are today, and she even had her own theatre and railway station built to receive people in style.

## By the sea

One of Harry's favourite places is Tenerife. "My mum knows someone who has an apartment there so we go and stay sometimes. There's a swimming pool, a water park and a jungle park." Harry also likes camping at Newgale in Pembrokeshire. "The waves are huge and only my friend and I are brave enough to go in the sea!"

## Family visits

Harry has family in England. His father lives in London and when he goes to see him, they visit the Natural History Museum and the Science Museum. He often visits his grandmother in Ludlow. His grandmother has a huge lawn at the back of the house where Harry and his cousin from Manchester have fun playing with his gran's two Dalmatian dogs.

## Mountain biker

Up in Ludlow, Harry goes mountain biking and practises a lot on a downhill track. "You climb all the way up this big hill, but when you go down it, you feel it's worth all the pain." Once a year there's a mountain bike trial and Harry's the youngest person in the elite group, just below the experts. "It takes me 15 minutes 25 seconds to race the two miles, because I go really fast down the jumps." Harry wears a lot of protective gear when he's mountain biking. "I did think at the beginning – why do I need all this gear? But then I saw a person having an accident. He wasn't wearing any shoulder pads or anything and he broke his neck. So I realised that you do need to protect yourself." Mountain biking teaches him to be alert, too – "You've got to concentrate on the track or you'll crash into a tree!"

# Llinos

| | |
|---|---|
| **age** | 8 |
| **birthday** | May |
| **home** | Wrexham, Denbighshire |
| **family** | parents and brother, 14 and sister, 11 |
| **interests** | computer games, shopping, reading, drawing, jigsaws and her dog, Ben |

*"It's not all bad being the youngest, though sometimes I do get a bit spoiled."*

## Family life

Llinos's mum works as a classroom assistant and her dad is a long-distance lorry-driver. Because he has to drive over to Ireland and Europe, he is often away from home. Llinos says she really misses him. "I miss having someone to tease and play tricks on. I like to sneak up behind him and jump out to give him a fright! It's nice when he comes back. He usually brings me sweets."

Llinos's family all speak Welsh at home. Although she goes to a Welsh school, there are only three or four children in her class from a Welsh-speaking home. Every summer, she goes to stay with her granny who lives in the heart of the countryside near Capel Garmon, where she meets her three Welsh cousins, Gethin, Sioned and Ceri, and Nain's dogs, Pero and Twm.

"We all have a lot of fun together," says Llinos. "Nain has a huge garden, and last summer we made a den down the hill with leaves and trees. It's a good place for hiding. Going to Nain's is my best thing of all."

*Llinos*

## School

Llinos likes school, especially playtime with her four best friends. Sometimes, if they've been singing really

well, or if it's sunny, they are allowed to play for a few extra minutes. Maths and technology are her favourite subjects, and she also enjoys PE and swimming. "But I don't like writing stories," she says. "That's quite hard."

Recently, Llinos went to Gulliver's World in Warrington on a school trip. "My favourite thing was the little train. It goes all round the park, and you can see all the rides. The only one that scared me a bit was the canoe boat because when you come down the water splashes all over you and you get soaked."

## What Llinos enjoys doing

✔ playing Harry Potter games on the computer, either on her own or with Leah

✔ going shopping in Wrexham's bustling shopping centre. "My favourite shop is Claire's Accessories and I love getting things for my hair."

✔ playing with her dog, Ben, and taking him for walks with her brother. "Ben's terrible for chewing things. We only just managed to get Dyfed's shoes away from him before they were ruined. He even tried to chew my teddy! We have to put things away upstairs."

✔ drawing all sorts of things, but especially Ben – when he's lying still outside. "Dyfed likes drawing too, and my mum is doing her GCSE in art at the school where she works."

✔ doing jigsaws with her mum and Nain – ones with 500 pieces

✔ reading books like *Harry Potter and the Prisoner of Azkaban*. She says that in school, she reads a lot of Welsh books too. "Sometimes I buy books, and sometimes I borrow them from the library. I like non-fiction as well as stories, and I like books with jokes in them."

*Here's one of Llinos's favourite jokes:*

**Q.** Why did the dogs sit by the fire?
**A.** Because they wanted to be hot dogs!

## And what she doesn't like doing

✘ falling over and hurting herself
✘ her mum going to town without her
✘ not being able to use the computer
✘ being shouted at by her brother

## What makes her particularly happy

As well as visiting Nain and going to school, Llinos enjoys good weather "as long as it's not too sunny. I got sunburned once and it was horrible." She loves collecting things, too.

"I collect the toys from Kinder eggs, and I have a collection of miniature animals that Nain gave me. I keep them all in a box in my bedroom."

And when Llinos grows up, she says: "I'd like to do something with horses. I really like horses, even though I've only been on one short ride when I was at Nain's. My mum told me that her dad once used to ride horses a lot."

## Did you know?

● that your breakfast this morning might have come from Wrexham? Kellogg's, the American company which makes cornflakes, All-Bran, Frosties and Coco-pops, has been manufacturing breakfast cereals there for over 25 years. After the cereals have been packaged, any waste cardboard is given to local playgroups and play schemes for craft projects. Maybe Llinos used some when she was in nursery school.

● that some people say that the cockerel on the Kellogg's cornflakes box was inspired by the Welsh word for cockerel, *ceiliog*, which sounds a bit like Kellogg if you say it quickly? It's said it was suggested by a Welsh harpist called Nansi Richards, who just happened to be staying with the Kellogg family in America at the time they were designing the carton.

● that you can see one of the traditional Seven Wonders of Wales in Wrexham? Find it in this rhyme:

*Pistyll Rhaeadr and Wrexham steeple,*
*Snowdon's mountains without its people,*
*Overton yew trees, St. Winefride's well,*
*Llangollen bridge and*
*Gresford bells.*

It's not really a steeple, though – St. Giles's church has a 140-foot-high tower. And Wrexham has another, older American link. If you ever go to Yale University in New Haven, Connecticut, you can see an identical tower in the quadrangle there. That's because the college was founded in 1701 by Elihu Yale, whose family came from the Wrexham area. You can see his tomb in St. Giles's church.

You can find out more about the Seven Wonders on: www.Welshdragon.net/resources/Historical/wonders.shtml

If you had to list your own Seven Wonders of Wales for the 21st century, what would you choose?

THIS STONE REPLACES ONE PRESENTED TO YALE UNIVERSITY, U.S.A. 1918.

# Arfon

| | |
|---|---|
| **age** | 9 |
| **birthday** | April |
| **home** | a small hillside village, halfway between Merthyr and Pontypridd |
| **family** | parents and brothers 11 and 12 |
| **interests** | his parrot, 'Gameboy', computer, cycling and playing with friends |

**"***I'm a happy-go-lucky sort of person, really. Maybe I do talk too much at school sometimes, but we should be allowed to ask questions about things, like what to do next, or about God, or spelling something.***"**

## Arfon's family

Arfon's family on his father's side come from Cornwall. His great-grandfather came to south Wales after the First World War to look for work. He found a job in a Phurnacite plant making smokeless fuel, and married and settled down in the Cynon valley.

"My Grancha – dad's dad – has just died, and we're all going to miss him lots. My Granny still lives by us, and my other Grancha and Granny live nearby as well. Mam's mother comes from Switzerland and she can speak French, German and English – but only me and Rhys speak Welsh in our family. They're all very proud of us. Because Mam and Dad wanted us to be real Welsh boys, they gave the three of us proper Welsh names. Rhys goes to big school now, and Dafydd goes to a special school because he's autistic. Dad used to be the one who stayed home to look after us, but now he works for three hours as a cleaner every day. And he's great at gardening; you should see our garden. And Mam's training to be a social worker in Merthyr, with children who need help. She says it's easier for women than for men to find work where we live."

## Housework

"I like helping in the house. Saturday mornings, I clean, polish and hoover my room, and sometimes other rooms too. For this, I get £1 pocket money. Once, I got £5 because Mam said the cleaning was excellent. And I can make tea. I love tea, and I take a cuppa to my bedroom. Mam says it's important to have skills. But she won't let me have a bank account yet."

## Pets

Arfon has an elderly dog called Megan, two gerbils, a goldfish in a pool in the garden and a ten-month-old parrot. "He was the only thing I wanted for Christmas. He's called Captain Carhart, after this sea-captain who 'belonged' to us. There's this story that he was shipwrecked and drowned in a storm, somewhere off the coast of Maryland in America in 1799. They say his grave is still there. I'm teaching the parrot to talk now, in Welsh and English."

## And how about school?

Arfon says he loves school, especially taking part in assemblies and drama.

"Once, I played a turkey, and we've got this video of me flapping and going gobble-gobble. Last Christmas, I was a beggar-boy. I had to wear rags. And I belong to the Urdd and I've been to Llangrannog and take part in folk-dancing and sports for the Eisteddfod. I never mind if we don't win."

Arfon also plays rugby for the school. "I usually play wing, because I can run fast, and I've run for the school, too. I wish I could run as fast as Sonic the hedgehog. Or Guto Nyth Brân!"

In lessons, maths is Arfon's favourite subject, though he likes them all.

✔ "In Welsh, we had to write this story about a monster that was half a man and half an animal and ate human flesh and lived in a maze. It was called the Minotaur. I had good marks because I remembered so much detail."

✔ "In history, we learned about Trevithick's steam engine up in Merthyr, and about the bet between Crawshay and Homfray."

✔ "In art, I've drawn a picture of my parrot."

The school has a 'buddy system' in which Year Six pupils look after the younger pupils and try to prevent bullying and encourage them to speak Welsh. Arfon always tries to help the buddies because he doesn't like bullying.

## Happy-go-lucky!

Arfon says he's nearly always a cheerful sort of person. He likes going out on his bike and playing with his friends round the village, and going for walks with the family.

"We go up the mountain, where there used to be a coal-mine once, though now the tips are all green. And I love holidays. In Corfu once we saw people dancing and jumping through fire, and we had shark to eat. And I like reading the jokes and riddles in the *Horrible History* books. And I feel really, really happy when I've done something good in school or at home."

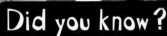

## Did you know?

- Arfon's home area once echoed with the clatter and roar of heavy industry. Thousands of people came to the valleys of the rivers Cynon and Taff to work in the ironworks and coal-mines. Tons of iron and coal were carried down the valleys by canal to Cardiff docks. And d'you know what? In 1804, the first steam engine of its kind in the world to run on an iron track chuffed down from Penydarren, Merthyr Tydfil to the Basin in Abercynon. The man who invented it was Richard Trevithick, who like Arfon, had Cornish connections.

- **Two proud men and their bet**
Samuel Homfray was so sure that Trevithick's steam engine would transport the iron much quicker than the canal that he bet Richard Crawshay, another of the rich owners of the ironworks, £1050 that he would be proved right. And of course, he was!

- **And who was Guto Nyth Brân?**
Guto was a very fast runner who came to a tragic end, and who is remembered in a race held every New Year's Eve in the Mountain Ash area. Try www.rhondda-cynon-taff.gov.uk and search for Guto Nyth Brân if you'd like to know more about him.

# Siân

| | |
|---|---|
| age | 10 |
| birthday | July |
| home | a house on a hill outside Prestatyn, Flintshire |
| family | parents and sister, 12 and brother 2 |
| interests | birdwatching, cooking, reading, singing and collecting things |

Siân x

*"It's our dream home. It's right at the top of a hill and looks down across Prestatyn and Meliden. We can see right over to Anglesey. If it's really clear, you can see all the way to Puffin Island. It's a view that always makes me feel happy."*

## "Our dream home"

Siân and her family moved to their hill-top home just over a year ago.

The family have a derelict cottage in their back garden. "I think it's a bit creepy," says Sian. "There are woods, too, behind us which lead to the 'fish caves'. I love going exploring there with my friends but you have to be really careful because there's a 150-foot drop at the end."

## Siân's family

Siân's mum is a theatre nurse in a hospital and her dad works for the police service. Sometimes he has to travel to other cities in Britain because he works for the Black Police Association.

Siân's grandparents and most of Siân's relatives on her mother's side live nearby in Prestatyn, but she also has a grandma in Trinidad, where her father comes from. "I was born in London and I lived in Trinidad for a year, but I can't remember much about it because I was only seven months old," says Siân. "Then we came back to live in Wales. I've been back to Trinidad twice since then, once when I was seven and again this year. It's so exciting there. I love the hot weather. It's even hot when it rains! The sea is really crystal-clear. Everyone swims – we can jump off the boats. Everything is so green. I love the steel pans and the calypso music, too.

I love seeing my grandma in Trinidad. She's wrinkly and fun to be with. Nobody knows how old she is, not even my dad. I often speak to her on the phone and she misses us because we're her only grandchildren. But I'm sad that Grandpa in Trinidad died before I was born.

My Nana in Prestatyn is a special person too. I see her two or three times a week and we do all sorts of things together, like cooking, shopping and crosswords."

## What Siân likes doing

✔**watching the birds…**
Sian's favourite room is the sun-lounge. "It's a great place for birdwatching," she explains. "I've got binoculars and a reference book to check their names. We get plenty of the common garden birds, but I've also spotted some of the more unusual birds such as a dunnock, treecreeper and nuthatch."

✔**being with her cat…**
"He's called TC, which can stand for anything depending on how he's behaving! Sometimes he can be Tiger Cat and sometimes Top Cat. TC likes to keep me company watching the birds – but he's too lazy to think of chasing them. I love him so much. He likes to rub his face against mine and give me a big hug – he's so sociable he's almost like a human."

✔**cooking…**
Siân loves helping to cook and can make spaghetti bolognese and cakes. She loves it when her dad is cooking. "He makes a fantastic curry," she says.

✔**reading…**
At the moment, Siân's favourite author is Michael Morpurgo. "I liked *Cool*, and loved *Kensuke's Kingdom* and *Out of the Ashes*."

✔**singing…**
Siân loves singing. Last year, she and Karys won a singing competition in a Youth Arts Festival in Prestatyn. "We sang 'All the things she said' by TATU. We were the only ones without microphones and the only two with a dance."

✔**collecting things …**
"for my special box, like my Trinidad prayer charm and a trinket casket from Rhys when he was born, and one of Karys's teeth!"

✔**School and friends…**
Sian loves school and especially her teacher Miss Robinson. "She's the best teacher in the whole world. She's fun, she makes me laugh and she sticks up for me," says Siân, who enjoys most subjects in school, though maths is her favourite.

## And what she doesn't like doing

Siân goes to weekly classes in Ju-jitsu, and she and Karys already have yellow belts. "Although I don't like going, Mum thinks self-defence is important so I'll keep going until I've managed to get my black belt."

## Siân feels angry

✘"when people tease me about my colour
✘when there's any kind of cruelty to animals or people
✘when forests and the environment are destroyed."

## Siân's best time ever

"It was when we went to Camelot for a surprise holiday. We thought we were just going somewhere for the day, and then we found Mum and Dad had booked us in. The roller-coasters were great!"

## And Siân's dreams for the future?

Siân would love to be a singer – that has been her dream since she was four. If she can't fulfil this dream she might like to be a fashion designer, or work in child care – perhaps even go into hairdressing. Whatever she does, she is sure to be enthusiastic and full of energy.

## Did you know?

● that the Welsh name for Puffin Island is 'Ynys Seiriol', which means Seiriol's island? Seiriol was a sixth-century saint who lived there on his own. It's said he used to walk from there to Penmaenmawr across Traeth Lafan, a bank of sand and marshland that may once have linked the island to the mainland. The island's English name refers to the huge number of puffins that used to nest there. But the numbers went down because so many were pickled in barrels of vinegar and spice, and eaten as a great delicacy.

# Jacob and Efan

| | |
|---|---|
| **age** | 11 |
| **birthday** | November |
| **home** | a house in a Vale of Glamorgan village |
| **family** | their parents |
| **interests** | rugby, soccer, music, drama, reading and telling jokes |

**Jacob** Sometimes it's a nuisance having someone who looks just like you, because you get blamed for something you haven't done.

**Efan** We don't always get on, but I wouldn't want to be without my twin.

Soon, the twins will be leaving their school in Maesteg, north of Bridgend, and moving to be nearer their secondary school in the Vale of Glamorgan.

**Jacob** We'll be able to stay for after-school clubs then. Mam and Dad are both headteachers, and it'll be much easier for them if we live nearer our school. We worry a bit about leaving our friends, though.

**Efan** We can always make new ones – and we can meet up with the others at weekends and holidays.

## What are the best things that have happened to the twins?

**Jacob** being on the telly for the launch of the school choir's CD, after we'd won a Radio Cymru carol competition.

**Efan** sitting in the best seats in the Millennium Stadium in Cardiff and seeing Wales playing Japan in the World Cup, and seeing Gareth Thomas scoring a try.

**Both** going to Disneyland, Florida, and going caravanning around Wales, England and France.

**Efan** Yeah – and finding funny words in other languages, like '*Oui!*' in French. Our den out in the garden of our new home is all right, too.

## And the worst?

**Efan** waiting half-an-hour while Jacob has his piano lesson.

**Jacob** waiting half-an-hour while Efan has his…and buying clothes.

## What about clothes?

**Efan** When we were small, we used to be dressed the same. But now, we can choose our own clothes outside school. I'm like Dad, I love looking in clothes shops, and being trendy, and putting gel and stuff on my hair.

**Jacob** *Ych-a-fi!* I hate shopping, full stop. Like Mam. And I can't even stand brushing my hair.

Jacob and Efan are identical twins. Jacob, the elder, was born nine minutes before Efan.

*Jacob*   *Efan*

## Pet animals?

**Jacob** We've got a cat called Siglen. And two rabbits, Arwen after the woman in *Lord of the Rings*, and Caradog because he was a Celtic warrior. They're allowed to come inside the house.

**Efan** And we've got two goldfish. Mine's called Nemo Simpson, and Jac's is called Montgomery.

## Interests?

✔ **rugby…**

**Jacob** I'm a flanker for the District Schools team, but I need to improve my tackling.

**Efan** I play wing and sometimes centre for them as well.

**Jacob** We train every Monday night and Saturday morning, as well as playing for another club on Sunday. We play for the school team too.

**Efan** I have a Christmas card signed by Shane Williams.

**Jacob** I have Ieuan Evans's autograph.

✔ **soccer...**

Efan's favourite team is Liverpool.

**Jacob** Mine is Man United. We've been to Old Trafford. I like watching football, but I'd rather play rugby.

**Efan** I like doing both.

✔ **then there's music...**

**Jacob** We have piano lessons after rugby training on Mondays, and in school, Efan has clarinet and I have flute and harp lessons.

**Efan** We sing in the school choir, too. The choir sang in the *plygain* in the church near our school.

✔ **and drama...**

**Jacob** I really liked acting part of this book called *Perthyn dim i'n teulu ni* (No relation to our family), and I had one of the main parts in the school show. I'm in the recitation party, too, and I like writing. I won a chair in the school eisteddfod for writing about my Grampy.

**Efan** One day the Mari Lwyd came to the school and a man with a horse's head came and sang outside and inside the door, and the horse's head had glass eyes, and a tweedy sort of cloth on its ears, and ribbons on its head.

✔ **and reading...**

**Jacob** I've taken part in the Reading Quiz lots of times. I've read *Ta ta Tryweryn*, a true story about drowning a village. I read a lot – books like *Lord of the Rings*, and Narnia stories, and I've bought thirteen of Enid Blyton's 'Secret Seven' series.

**Efan** I preferred the *Lord of the Rings's* films to the Harry Potter ones. They were scarier, and Frodo and Gollum were really well-acted.

✔ **and just messing about in their den...**

✔ **and telling jokes...**

**Jacob** Knock knock.
Who's there?
Astra.
Astra who?
Hastra-la vista, baby!

**Efan** Knock knock.
Who's there?
Police.
Police who?
Per-leese let me in – it's cold outside!

## The twins feel miserable when...

**Jacob** I've done everything right, like asking nicely for a turn on the computer, and nobody takes any notice, and that's really not fair.

**Efan** someone winds me up because I've let a ball through in the goal... maybe someone who's been selected for the school team, and thinks he's great...

## And they are angry about the fighting in Iraq.

**Jacob** Perhaps one day someone will write something like *Hitler's Hideout* about the place where they found Saddam Hussein.

## And if they won a million pounds?

**Efan** I'd buy a racing car, a Honda McLaren F1, and have a mansion built of solid gold. And have any food I wanted.

**Jacob** I'd put half of it in the bank. And give a quarter to a charity for cancer research, because Gran has had cancer, and I'd use the rest to go to Austria, or Australia and Germany – to see things about the history of the Second World War.

# Robert

| | |
|---|---|
| **age** | 9 |
| **birthday** | January |
| **home** | a small village near Corwen, Denbighshire |
| **family** | his parents and sisters aged 11 and 4 |
| **interests** | football, reading and writing in Braille, music and cycling |

*"On our school trip to Drayton Manor we had to queue for an hour-and-a-half to go on Storm Force 10 – then I found out you could go to the front of the queue if you were blind!"*

## What he likes doing

Though Robert is blind, this does not stop him from enjoying most of the same activities as his friends. He especially likes playing football with them.

"I support Manchester United. I've got a football with metal bearings in it which makes it easier for me to find. I like going swimming, too. I'm really good at the torpedo (it's like front crawl) and I've just completed the Bronze Award. In the summer I love playing cricket; I can hear where the ball is because it's got a bell in it. In the school sports I entered all the races. In the hurdles Auntie Nerys ran with me and every time I came to a hurdle, she told me to jump but I still managed to knock them all down."

## Robert's family

Robert's mum works in a local old people's home and his dad is a landscape gardener. Robert has lived in the village all his life and most of his cousins, uncles and aunts also live in the village or nearby.

"In our family, we have a lot of parties for special occasions like weddings, anniversaries and special birthdays. These are always really good. One of my best days ever was Gareth and Claire's wedding, when I stayed up really late with all my cousins. We were dancing till half-past-eleven!"

Robert gets on well with his sisters. "Kate is good at telling me what's going on when we're watching TV or at the cinema, and Emily helps me and shares her sweets with me. She's quite good at football, too, like Ben, my dog, though he sometimes bursts the footballs with his teeth."

Robert enjoys going on holiday with his family in their caravan and tent to places like Porthmadog, Tenby, Newcastle, Devon and especially Pwllheli, where there were lots of activities.

FROSTIES
ASA AWARDS SCHEME
BRONZE

CHALLENGE AWARD

## Books

Robert enjoys reading very much. "I've read all of the Harry Potter books and so far the fifth is the best. I've listened to *The Lord of the Rings* by J.R.R. Tolkien and I like anything by Enid Blyton, Roald Dahl and Margaret Mahy. I like poetry too. A really good poetry book is *Thawing Frozen Frogs* by Brian Patten. My books are all written in Braille. I get them from my local library in Corwen. I also get some sent to me from the NLB (National Library for the Blind) and Welsh books from RNIB Cymru. Braille is easy to learn to read and write."

## Writing stories

Robert writes poems as well as stories on his 'Brailler'. "I had first prize for my story and poem at the school eisteddfod in March. My poem was about one of my friends. Anytime I have five minutes, I try to write something."

## Other things Robert enjoys

✔ **music…**
He plays the piano, recorder and French horn, and enjoys istening to pop bands.

✔ **cycling…**
As well as having his own bike, Robert has a tandem that he rides on with his dad. "I used to fall off my bike a lot, but now I'm much better and I can do turns."

✔ **food!**
Robert loves food, but he has to follow a special low-fat diet. "It makes me annoyed. I can't eat much chocolate and I'm not allowed fish and chips or MacDonald's either. But I am allowed my favourite meal – chicken casserole – and some of my favourite puddings like apple crumble, apple tart and spotted dick. And Turkish Delight."

✔ **the Urdd Eisteddfod…**
"It's really good fun and we do lots of things for the Eisteddfod at my school. This year in the Art and Craft I did a 2D picture that came second in the Urdd National Eisteddfod. I came second too in the County Eisteddfod for reciting 'Smotiau'. I was more nervous, though, at the Eisteddfod Gylch in Llangollen."

## School life

Robert hates having to stay home if he's not feeling well. He loves school, and has lots of friends who help him and play with him. He likes lessons, especially maths, Welsh and English, and says he's looking forward to doing French in High School. "Our school is linked with a school in Nepal and both my sister and I have pen friends there. I write to them about twice each term and we've raised money to help them build their school. Two of our teachers have visited Nepal and so they can tell us a lot about it."

## When Robert grows up

He wants to be an author. "If not, my mam says I could be a lawyer. I'd really like to do something where I could use my voice."

## Did you know?

● Corwen was a centre for cattle-drovers, who used to gather there at the crossing of the river Dee on the way to sell their livestock in English markets. But it's better known as the base for the fifteenth-century warrior, Owain Glyndŵr. Not far away is the site of the house where he used to live, and where he was proclaimed Prince of Wales by his supporters. There's a statue of him in Corwen.

● Valle Crucis Abbey in the Dee valley just outside Llangollen used to be very famous for its good food and friendly welcome. A Welsh poet called Gutyn Owain praised the Abbot and said it was like Christmas all the year round there, with all the free feasts. Robert would surely have enjoyed the celebrations!

● If you go to Llangollen in July, you'll see that the town still gives a warm welcome to people from all over the world at the Llangollen International Musical Eisteddfod. Every year since 1947 people have been coming there to sing and dance, usually in colourful national dress.

● It was the Frenchman Louis Braille who invented a way of printing letters so they could be read by touch. The RNIB now have all kinds of reading material – books, music, bills, exam papers – available in braille.

# Emily

| | |
|---|---|
| **age** | 11 |
| **birthday** | January |
| **home** | a house near the sea in Pembrokeshire |
| **family** | lives with her mother |
| **interests** | sailing and other water sports, sea creatures, beach-combing |

## Happy memories...

Emily's grandfather used to be in the family business, but he died recently. Emily was close to her grandfather.

"One of the fondest memories of my grandfather is going to his house when both he and Nanny were still alive and having tea and staying the night with them. I used to call my grandfather 'Damps' and when I think of him, I remember all the good times we had and how he made me laugh."

## Caring for animals...

Not surprisingly, Emily loves sea animals and likes visiting a local seal sanctuary where baby seals are taken if they are ill or after being rescued from the sea. They have swimming pools and toys to play with, and when they get better, they are released back into the sea.

Emily gets really angry if she sees anything on television where people are being cruel to animals. "When I'm older, I'd like to work with animals, but not as a vet because I wouldn't want to see them die," she says.

## All at sea...

Emily really loves living on the coast and enjoys many water sports activities. She has been sailing since she was four and also goes kayaking, swimming, windsurfing and coasteering. "To go coasteering you have to wear a wetsuit and a helmet," Emily explains. "You climb along the rocks, but keep above sea level."

Emily is an only child, but has lots of friends and family living close by. She says that she's really happy when she's swimming or doing her water sports activities when they are there too.

Emily's mother runs a windsurfing and sailing school, and the family also organises boat trips to the islands of Skomer and Skokholm. Emily loves going out on the boat as well, although she can remember one occasion when she was glad to come home.

"Once there was a storm when we were on the boat, and we had a bad time. I started to worry whether we'd get back home in one piece. But looking back, it was one of the best experiences I've ever had."

## Favourite things...

✔Emily likes collecting pebbles and worn pieces of glass from the beach and has them on display in the bathroom at home. These are some of her 'treasures'.

✔"I also have a necklace my Nan gave me, and I still have some cuddly toys from when I was small."

✔Apart from Pembrokeshire, Emily's favourite places are France and Greece, but her ideal place is "anywhere where it's nice and sunny".

## Days indoors...

At home, Emily enjoys reading some of the Harry Potter books. She doesn't watch much TV, but she does enjoy *Eastenders*, some cartoons and films. She sometimes plays computer games: *Sims*, which is about designing people and their houses and running their lives for them, and *Cybertime*, which involves masked and history games.

Emily's favourite instrument is the recorder, which she learned to play at school. The lessons she likes best are English, art and drama and she's really looking forward to studying art in secondary school, as well as making new friends there.

## The future...

At the moment, Emily works in the shop and café that the family run. She helps behind the till and serves the customers in the café. "I think I'm better at sums because of working behind the till. And I also get used to talking to other people."

While she's growing up, Emily is looking forward to having a job and being responsible for things. She also likes babies, and would like to be a mother one day. But whatever she does when she's older, she'll probably be living near the sea!

## Did you know?

● that Skomer and Skokholm were given their names by the Vikings and Danes who swept around the Welsh coast in the ninth century?

● that the islands are National Nature Reserves famous for their protected wildlife and birds – seagulls and kittiwakes, puffins, choughs and gannets?

Perhaps, one day, you'll be able to sail over to Skomer and Skokholm. If you're there in late summer or autumn, you might see white-furred seal pups. Perhaps there will be dolphins and porpoises playing in the tide race – and perhaps, if you go to Skomer at dusk, and you are very lucky (and very quiet), you will hear the extraordinary screech of the 160,000 Manx shearwaters which live on the island. The Manx shearwater is a very shy bird which lives in old rabbit warrens. It prefers to feed its family in the dark to avoid being bullied by other birds. Once you've heard it, you'll never forget the unearthly squawking of the thousands of Manx sheerwaters. Aaaaargh…

● On a clear day, maybe Emily can see the island of Grassholm. Grassholm is like a little round button far away in the west. This is the enchanted island – called Gwales in Welsh – which is mentioned in the old Welsh legends called the Mabinogi. Read the second tale to find out why seven warriors stayed there for 80 years in the company of their leader Bendigeidfran's head – or what about enjoying it on animated film?

# Simeon

| | |
|---|---|
| **age** | 10 |
| **birthday** | September |
| **home** | Denbigh in north-east Wales |
| **family** | parents, three brothers and one sister |
| **interests** | football, reading, the computer, watching films, and playing the piano |

## Simeon's family

Simeon's family are Catholics and all go to church on Sundays. Simeon is the youngest member of the family. His eldest brother, Samuel, is away travelling in India and Granada and teaching English. Miriam, his sister, is in a sixth-form college, and Dominic and Gabriel, his other two brothers, are both at school. Simeon's mum has recently finished training to become a social worker, and his dad is a psychiatrist.

The family lives in Denbigh, a medieval walled town with the ruins of a splendid Norman castle perched on a hill-top, looking out over the Vale of Clwyd and the Clwydian mountains. Steep narrow lanes lead to their house, which used to be a girls' school. "At the top, it's got a circle window that used to be a clock," says Simeon. "It's one of the highest points in town."

## Job rotas

Because they are a big family, they have a rota for jobs like setting the table, washing up and taking the compost out.

"That's the job I hate most of all - it smells," says Simeon. "And we have a rota for taking our dog, Moses, for a daily walk. We take him to Snowdonia every Saturday, to places like Betws-y-coed, or up Siabod, which was the first mountain he ever climbed. He did get half-way up Snowdon, but it got too misty. Moses's favourite things are eating and sleeping, but most of all, he likes water and swimming in waterfalls like the one at Llanrhaeadr. My own pet is Coco, a guinea-pig. He takes quite a bit of time to look after. I have to feed him, clean out his cage and play with him."

## Family holidays

Usually, the family go camping. They have to take three tents. Often, they go to the Pyrenees in Spain. "We do lots of walking. I like it best when there's a fun part at the end, like a scree run. We like caves too," explains Simeon.

## School

"School is okay. The subjects I enjoy most are art, English (especially story-writing), technology, PE and IT," says Simeon. "The main thing I like about school is seeing my friends. I don't have one special friend but I'm friends with a lot of the boys, and mostly just see them in school. I'm always sad when one of my friends moves away."

## Simeon is always happy when he's...

✔ playing and writing stories on the computer

✔ playing football, his favourite sport, with his friends and in matches against other schools. "My favourite team is Liverpool and my favourite player is Steven Gerrard. I've got some of the team posters."

✔ reading, mostly fiction and especially fantasy. Simeon has read all except two Harry Potter books. "I like the author Tamora Pierce, too. My favourite book, which I've read three or four times is *The Mahabarata*, an Indian story about two royal families that go to war."

✔ playing the piano, but he says he doesn't practise every day.

✔ watching films and DVDs, though the family doesn't have television. "Sometimes at weekends we rent a film. My favourites are adventure and comedy, like 'Red Dwarf'."

✔ and sometimes, cooking. The

family are all vegetarians. "I quite like cooking, but only cakes, not savoury meals. If I bake, I like to make a plain sponge. My favourite meals are pizza, pasta and chips. I don't mind lentils, but I prefer them with something."

And he's especially happy when it's Friday, and when Liverpool wins!

## But he feels angry when...

✘ "I have a fight with one of my brothers"

✘ "I get the blame for something I haven't done (often just because I'm the youngest)."

✘ "I have to come off the computer, or when I'm playing football and I have to come in and get changed."

✘ "politicians make bad decisions, like bombing other countries, or not banning things like hunting tigers and cutting down rain forests."

## And when Simeon grows up...

he would like to be an actor or an author, and live near the sea "where there's nice, warm weather, maybe around the Caribbean or the Mediterranean. I'd like to be successful in whatever I eventually do, and hopefully, get quite rich, too!"

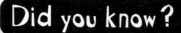

● that the famous words "Dr. Livingstone, I presume?" were uttered by a man who was born in 1841 in a cottage near Denbigh Castle? His name was John Rowlands, but he changed it later on to the much grander name of Henry Moreton Stanley. After escaping from the workhouse in St. Asaph where he'd been brought up, he went to Liverpool. There he became a cabin boy on a ship going to New Orleans. In America, he found a rich benefactor, who helped H.M. Stanley to become a celebrated journalist and explorer. In 1869, he was sent to find Dr. David Livingstone in east Africa. Dr. Livingstone was a Scottish missionary and explorer in that part of Africa, and nothing had been heard of him for a long time. After travelling hundreds of miles, and some hair-raising adventures, Stanley found him near Lake Tanganyika. He was so relieved to see Livingstone that he just took off his hat and said: "Dr. Livingstone, I presume?" A mobile phone could have saved a lot of trouble for everybody!

● that in medieval times, Denbigh was the scene of many fierce battles between the Welsh and the Norman invaders? Its name in Welsh means 'little fortress' and it lies halfway between Rhuthun and Rhuddlan castles, right on the warpath of the Norman and Welsh armies and part of the mighty chain of castles built by Edward 1 to subdue the Welsh. Today, though, you'd feel quite safe there - the only 'invaders' are the tourists who come to see the castle and perhaps walk the town trail.

● Another Denbigh 'celeb' was Thomas Gee, who set up his printing works in the town in the nineteenth century. Gee was a famous printer, publisher and editor, whose strong views made people think hard. Lively Welsh newspapers, magazines, journals, dictionaries, and collections of sermons and poetry poured into Welsh homes from the Gee Press, making it a household name in Wales at a time when there was no radio or television.

# Serena

| | |
|---|---|
| **age** | 9 |
| **birthday** | May |
| **home** | Hay-on-Wye, a small town on the border between Wales and England |
| **family** | parents and brothers, 31 and 11 |
| **interests** | reading, writing, crafts, choir and netball |

*"I know heaven's up in the sky but I'm not really sure what it's like there. I just wonder what it would be like to be dead. I'd be able to see everybody, but they wouldn't be able to see me. If anyone wondered if I was a ghost, I'd go: 'Yes, I'm here!'"*

Serena

"I live with my mum and dad and Daniel, who is eleven, and I have another brother, Aeron, who's 31. I weighed just one pound and fourteen ounces when I was born, so I had to spend a long time in an incubator to keep me safe and help me grow bigger. I wonder what it was like being in an incubator. I imagine it was scary being all wired up and having all these tubes going in and out. Because I was such a good little baby, they called me Serena. It's a name which comes from the English word 'serene', which means calm and placid. Now, I'm nearly as tall as Daniel. Mum thinks that's because we've always eaten healthy foods.

## Me and my brothers

Daniel and I sometimes have fights about who goes on the Playstation. But I know that when I go up to the big school, Daniel will be there if someone bullies me. I like my big brother Aeron a lot because he's funny, like Dad. It'd be good if he lived here and not in London.

### Pets

I have a hamster called Albert, who's a bit boring because he only wakes up at night."

### The Town of Books

Hay is often called 'The Town of Books' because there are over 30 bookshops there. Serena's father sells second-hand books in the one he owns.

"I stay in Dad's shop when Mum goes to work. I like going there because I enjoy reading, and the shop has a lot of girls' annuals. I like reading fiction best, though sometimes I read factual books about animals. Once, I found this great book about all the animals in the world, even the microscopic ones.

### When I grow up...

I'd like to be an author because I enjoy writing stories. They're usually adventure and horror stories, like the Goosebumps series. The one I'm in the middle of now is about a werewolf. It was inspired by this book I borrowed from the library called *Write your own Chillers*.

### School

My school has an eco flag because we all help to look after the environment, like always picking up litter in the yard. I'm in Year Five, and I've won a prize for helping in the school fruit shop. Daniel has homework every night, but I only get homework on Fridays. I learn Welsh in school on Mondays and Wednesdays, though I'm not really fluent. I think everybody should learn Welsh in case somebody asks you a question in Welsh, because if you weren't able to answer, maybe they'd think you were being a bit rude.

What I've especially enjoyed at school was listening to *The War of the Worlds* by H.G. Wells on the radio. It really is quite good, all about what would happen if aliens came to our world. When it first came on the radio, everyone was really scared because they thought it was real. It could be. There might be things happening on Mars that we don't know about...

### O for Organic

Most of the food we eat at home is organic. That's food grown as it used to be long ago, without any chemicals. We have two gardens – one next to the bookshop – and an orchard, and we grow leeks and potatoes, marrows and pumpkins, broccoli, cabbage, lettuce, and cucumber. Oh, and lots of herbs. Mum is Irish, and she is a herbalist as well as working in a home for old people. She keeps the medicines she makes from the herbs in a special cabinet in the computer room and then when one of us is ill we have herb medicine instead of going to the doctor's.

### What I like doing...

✔ I'm quite creative and like making things from empty toilet rolls and things. After Mum taught me to knit I made a little cloak for my Pokémon tortoise.

✔ For Christmas, I got a disk with graphics to put on cards, posters and calendars and all sorts of things.

✔ I go to netball club, arts and crafts club, and choir as well.

✔ We always entertain the old people at Christmas in the local hotel.

## Did you know?

● It was a local man called Richard Booth who first had the idea of turning Hay into a town of books. It was he who opened the first second-hand bookshop there in 1961. By today, the town has over a million books for sale. Mr. Booth owns Hay castle, too, and he's sometimes called 'King of Hay'. You can visit the castle, and buy a book at the shop there.

● One of the world's most famous book festivals is held in Hay every year. It's a kind of 'Olympics' for readers and writers, but without the competitions. People who like reading and writing come from all over the world to listen to poets and writers talking about their work, and the children's book events are very popular.

● In the past, people depended all the time on medicines made from local herbs and plants? Long ago, the Physicians of Myddfai in south Wales were famous for using them to help people get well.

I get 50p pocket money a week. I can earn more if I help with the housework. I sometimes spend it on cakes from the baker's, but I like to save up for something big.

### If I had three wishes

I really wish the fighting in Iraq would stop. I'm not sure about being famous or rich because I'd have reporters everywhere. I'd like Mum to be a bit younger, because she says she's quite ancient. And I'd like it if one of my stories came true – as long as it's not the one about the werewolf!"

# Luke

| age | 9 |
|---|---|
| birthday | March |
| home | a village on the Anglesey side of the Menai Straits |
| family | parents and brother, 5 |
| interests | oyster-hunting, riding, clarinet, cycling and drawing |

*"I always think Anglesey people are different from the rest of the people of Wales – that's because they all speak Welsh!"*

Luke

Luke does always speak Welsh to his mother and to his little brother Ioan. But when he talks to his father and Grandad, his father's father, who comes from Holland, he always speaks in English.

## Walking to school

Even though Ioan is only in the reception class at the moment, he and and his big brother Luke always walk together to school and back and wouldn't dream of going by car. "Well, it's really not very far anyway," says Luke. "Usually Ioan and I are fine together. He can be a bit naughty, though, and sometimes we argue about who gets to use the Playstation."

## Clarinet

Luke loves playing the clarinet. "I performed in a duet with my friend in a harvest festival service recently in chapel. Mam used to play the cello when she was in school, so I suppose music's bound to be in my genes. I'm glad, though, that the clarinet's a lot smaller and much easier to carry around than a cello."

## Titch

Titch the sheepdog lives on Luke's Nana and Grandad's farm. Luke says his Nana rescued Titch years ago and that he's always been perfectly happy living in a shed outside, and hardly ever comes into the house. "Even though he's about fifteen years old, he still loves coming for a walk with me, and I love taking him too. But he has to be kept on a lead because by now he's stone deaf and there'd be no point in calling him if he got lost because he wouldn't be able to hear you!"

## Riding – horses as well as bikes

Luke is a very good artist, but when he isn't painting and drawing he often goes cycling, or to a nearby equestrian centre. "The horse I usually ride is called Dandy," explains Luke. "She's huge, but she's gentle, too. I wear a helmet and special gloves and I always feel safe when I'm with Dandy. There's a horse in the field at the back of our house as well. He's a stallion called Microchip. No-one would really want to ride him because he's so small and grubby. And though he's supposed to be a white stallion, you'd never think he was white, because he loves rolling in the mud so much he looks more like a dirty toffee colour. And he adores apples and polo mints."

## Pizza in a box

Luke says his favourite food is definitely pizza. "I prefer the kind that comes in a box, not the one that Mam makes, and tuna's my favourite topping." He also likes fish and every kind of seafood – especially mussels – which is fortunate, considering what his dad does for a living!

## Oyster and mussel farming

In a way, you could describe Luke's dad as a farmer on the Menai Straits, the river-like channel which separates the island of Anglesey from the mainland. Instead of raising sheep or cows to sell, though, he farms mussels and oysters to supply the food trade.

Sometimes Luke goes with his father in their boat along the straits, where they gather the mussels. They use a dredge, which is a metal frame with a net on the back, to scrape mussels off the seabed.

The oysters grow nearer the shore, and when the tide is out, Luke and his dad are able to collect them without having to use the boat.

The Menai Straits is a good place for oysters. In fact, Luke's father discovered the largest oyster ever found in Europe, and his find has been recorded in *The Guiness Book of Records*.

Just imagine, perhaps the next plate of mussels you'll eat will have come from the Menai Straits via Luke's dad!

## Hunting for pearls

Maybe, when you prise open an oyster, you'll be lucky enough to find a pearl inside.

"Dad and I have found quite a lot of tiny white pearls inside some of the shells and we keep them in a little

glass pot on the mantelpiece," says Luke. "They're not really worth much, not like the huge ones they find in other parts of the world. But they are still beautiful."

## The best nurse in the world

The little jar of seed pearls reminds the family of the interesting and important work that Luke's father does. But it's not only his dad who works. His mother also has a very important job; she works as a nurse at a hospital in Bangor. Whenever Luke is unwell, he feels glad to have a nurse as a mother. "I think my dad's the best fisherman on the Straits, and my mum's the best nurse in the world."

## Did you know?

● that if you were a fish, you'd have an excellent time in the Menai Straits, with plenty of the right kind of fish food and lots of interesting companions? Partly because of the tide race and its currents, and partly for other environmental reasons, the straits have an underwater world which is home to many rare creatures as well as sea bass, conger eels and cod. But you'd have to watch out for marine biologists from Bangor University who might want to pickle you for study!

● that in the autumn you might visit the Oyster Festival in Trearddur Bay, where you can eat oysters and mussels to your heart's content?

● that before the two bridges over the Menai Straits were built people had to cross by ferry boat? Large animals, such as cows and horses, were led out over sandbanks and just had to swim through the deepest parts!

# Sophie

*"We have the best mum ever. She does everything for us. She keeps us clean and gives us healthy food like fruit and pasta and veg and tuna jacket potato. She's always wanted to go to Paris and if I won the lottery I'd send her there."*

Sophie

| | |
|---|---|
| age | 9 |
| birthday | May |
| home | a house on an estate near Llanelli, Carmarthenshire |
| family | parents and 4 sisters aged 12, 4 (twins) and 2 |
| interests | rugby, netball, cycling, violin and playing with friends |

## A large family

Sophie enjoys being a member of a very large local family. She has two older step-sisters and three young nephews as well as her four sisters. Her mother's father lives just up the road.

"Dad-cu speaks Welsh, like my other gran and great-gran who live in Pontarddulais. I can't speak Welsh very well myself, though. I love my Dad-cu. He's been ill and he can't work now. But because my dad's away a lot and my mam works, Dad-cu's always there for us. He takes me rugby training, and looks after his own family too."

## All girls together

Sophie shares a bedroom with the twins, Chloe and Danielle, and two-year-old Jorja. "All my clothes and toys are there, so my friends can play with me. But the little ones have all their stuff downstairs," says Sophie.

All the girls have to do jobs for their pocket-money. Jessica, the eldest, is responsible for clearing up in the kitchen, and the twins have to look after and clear away their toys. Sophie gets £2 a week for making her bed, opening the curtains and tidying up.

## School breakfast

Apple juice and toast and fruit or yogurt – that's what Sophie has for breakfast in school. "School dinners are a bit better now, but I suppose I'm a bit of a fussy eater really, and I don't like it when the hot dinners are put out on a plate before we get there, and it's cold."

## What Sophie does in school

Sophie is involved in lots of different school activities and is always happy playing rugby, netball, playing in the orchestra or singing with the choir. Mathematics is Sophie's favourite subject. She likes it so much that she bought a huge maths file full of old maths sheets for 20 pence from a past pupil.

"I can work out all the answers at home and then I can help my sisters," she says. Sophie thinks the world of her teacher, too. "She's strict and I respect that, but she's not bossy and she says 'Brilliant!' if you do something right."

## ✔Reference books

Finding out about things in reference books is something else that Sophie enjoys.

"I liked learning about smallpox, cowpox and milkmaids. I've learned that if you had what they called milkmaid spots – that's like white lumps, 20 pence in size – you'd never have smallpox. Milkmaids would develop these lumps after working with cows for years. A doctor called Jenner discovered inoculation and most doctors didn't believe him when he said that taking stuff from the milkmaid spots and giving it to other people would stop them having smallpox."

## ✔Rugby

As well as playing rugby in school, Sophie also plays at a local club during the week. "Mam pays every week for me. If it weren't for her, I wouldn't be able to go. Every week I do training, and on Sunday there's a game either home or away, at places like Mumbles or Pen-y-groes. I play forward in the second row. I'm good at the rucking. I was very proud this week because they said I was excellent. I used to be a bit scared but now, because I think I can do it, I really am better."

## ✔Weekends

When Sophie goes out to see friends who live nearby, she always has to tell her mother where she's going. If it's fine, she goes cycling with them on the beach path that goes round the coast to Pembrey Country Park, or maybe on a Saturday she'll go into town with her mum to Llanelli Market, and to choose clothes. Sometimes friends come to her house, and they play on the trampoline in the garden, or upstairs if it's wet. "I've got craft things from the Early Learning Centre, with lots of shells and figures and shapes, and we make pictures," says Sophie.

## ✔Family outings and holidays

Sometimes the family goes on a day trip to somewhere like Legoland in Windsor, or the wetlands park at Penclacwydd. Sophie says her best holiday was a fortnight on the Costa Brava. "We ate pancakes every morning for breakfast and I liked the food, though Mam's is better. And there were lots of activities: I won the hockey game and my uncle – who's eight! – won the football. And I learned Spanish words like *gracias* which means 'thank you' and *hola*, 'hello'.

## And when Sophie grows up

Her gran says Sophie ought to be a hairdresser or a singer. "I love karaoke and singing on stage, especially 'Country Roads' and Lizzie McGuire songs," says Sophie.

Perhaps one day, Sophie will be at the top of the pops chart!

## Did you know?

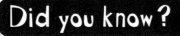

● that one of the most famous rugby songs of all time, 'Sosban Fach' is associated with Llanelli, which was once the British centre of the tinplate industry? Saucepans, cooking utensils, cans and boxes manufactured in local factories were sent all over the world from Llanelli docks. It's said that the goalposts in Stradey Park rugby ground are capped by cutouts of saucepans.

● that from Sophie's house you can see where the new stadium for the Scarlets rugby football team will be built? Sophie will have a marvellous view.

● that one of the largest television production companies in the UK outside London is based in Llanelli? It's called Tinopolis, the name Llanelli people used to call their town when the tin industry there was at its peak.

● that Tinopolis includes an animation department directed by Dave Edwards, the man who created Superted?

# Gruffudd

*"I love being with the animals on Taid and Nain's farm. And I like going to the National Library where my mum works to see pictures sometimes – and to slide on the shiny wooden floors!"*

Gruffudd

### At home with the family

Gruffudd always speaks Welsh with his parents and with Harri, his little brother, who enjoys football as well as ballet dancing. "But sometimes Harri says some words in English because by now there are more children in the reception class who don't speak Welsh than when I was there," says Gruffudd.

Because his father has a special post with the police force, Gruffudd is very aware of stories in the news. "I don't feel comfortable when I go into town and see people sitting around drinking or wearing untidy sort of clothes. But our village is a safe place as long as you take care when you're walking on the bridge, because of the traffic. One night, a lorry didn't make the corner, and it hit a car. I heard this terrific bang at three in the morning. I thought it must have been one of the cats!"

### Pet animals...

It's a good thing that Gruffudd is so fond of animals, because he and Harry share their home with seven of them. Here they are:
- 3 tom cats called Reg, Jac and Sid
- 3 goldfish called Iestyn, Idwal and Ifan
- 1 hamster called Caradog (who sleeps in Gruffudd's bedroom)

### ...and farm animals

When he's on the farm, Gruffudd always helps with the animals. One of his favourite memories is about the birth of a lamb. "We had to have straw to wipe the afterbirth off the lamb's nose, so that it could breathe, and then we gave it to its mother so that she could lick it clean. I felt so happy and proud that I was able to help it to be born. I wouldn't want to be a vet, though, because I don't really like the sight of blood. One day, I'd like to be a farmer. But there won't be any hens or ducks, in case a fox gets them."

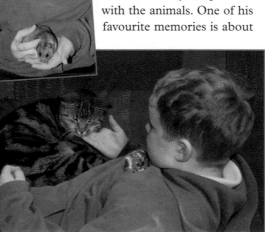

## Smaller birds and bigger ones

Gruffudd's other grandparents also have a farm, which is a habitat for eighty red kites. Gruffudd says that that was how he started to become interested in birds. Once a fortnight, the family goes birdwatching to Ynys-hir Nature Reserve, run by the RSPB.

"I've seen Canada geese, small birds like blue tits, and bigger ones like herons and storks."

## Fresh air

If he could, Gruffudd would spend all day and every day out-of-doors. When he's not on the farm or bird-watching, he plays rugby for Aberystwyth or for his school team, and football for the second team. He's won five medals for playing rugby, and last year, he won the Player of the Year's cup for his work as goalkeeper.

"We didn't have a family celebration," says Gruffudd. "I don't like a fuss. To tell the truth, I prefer rugby – you can get into the mud, and it's rougher. My heroes are Gareth Thomas, Dafydd Jones and Shane Williams, because they're such good players. But I don't like players who kick people."

## Striking a bargain

Gruffudd is always willing to help in the house. "If Mam's in a bad mood, I always notice. And I ask her if I can help."

Sometimes with some jobs, Gruffudd will strike a bargain. For example, if he's willing to hoover up the leaves in the garden, his mum and dad will agree to buy him a present. Hoovering up the leaves is quite a big job, which can take several days, so he banks the 'promise' until he has enough to buy a rugby shirt or a new football.

"I like cooking too. I like making spicy food like curry and chilli. Or I'll make a cake, or an apple tart."

## In school

By now, Gruffudd is very happy in school, but there was a time when he wasn't quite so happy.

"When I was in year 4, I was bullied. I told Mam and Dad to tell the teacher. The bullying stopped straight away after that."

Last year, Gruffudd came second in the school Eisteddfod for a poem about 'The Door'.

"I like reading funny books and poetry in English and in Welsh. I like Asterix too, and the Simpsons and Harry Potter. Tudur Dylan came to school when he was Children's Poet for Wales, and helped us to write poems for Hallowe'en. Our school has a magazine called *Cario Clecs*, which comes out once a year. We have to write three things, and then Mr Jones chooses one of them for the magazine."

## Family outings

Sometimes the family goes shopping in Machynlleth, or to the Alternative Technology Centre nearby. There, Gruffudd enjoys playing with the generator and going through the underground tunnel to see creatures and plant life underneath the earth. Occasionally, they go to see an exhibition in the National Library of Wales, where his mother is an Arts Officer. She looks after the valuable collection of pictures there.

"I saw the Paul Robeson exhibition, but not the one about John Charles," says Gruffudd. "It's hard to keep up with everything!"

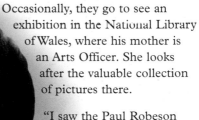

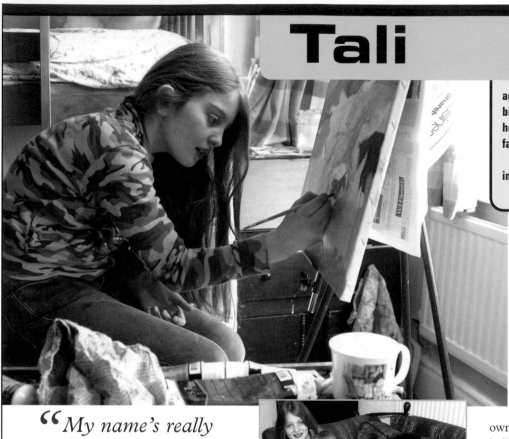

# Tali

| age | 9 |
|---|---|
| birthday | January |
| home | Newtown |
| family | brother, 7 and sister 3 – and baby, 3 months old |
| interests | horse riding, sewing, crafts and sport |

*Talitha.*

### Riding

Tali adores horse riding. It all started when she was put on a horse when she was about three or four. She now has lessons once a week and is saving up for her own horse, and her idea of heaven would be to be on her own in a field full of foals. "Dad says he'll double whatever I've saved at the end. Arabs are nice but a bit expensive, so I'll probably go for a Welsh mountain pony."

*❝My name's really Talitha, but everybody calls me Tali. I used to live in Hampshire, but Mum's Welsh so we moved to Wales when I was six. Hampshire was nice, but it's more beautiful here.❞*

### Tali's mum and dad

Tali's mum and dad met at art school. "My mum used to sell art before she started having babies," says Tali. "One day, she hopes to turn the garage into a studio, and start selling again. My dad started as an artist but then became so poor he went into business management but now he's a preacher! He loves it and I'm very proud of him. He can bring the Bible alive and help people understand the bits they couldn't understand before."

### Isaac and Isabelle

"My little brother Isaac is a brilliant artist and likes sport. We get on quite well, but not all the time! Isabelle likes 'piggies' – real ones – and singing and dancing. She chatters a lot and likes singing 'Twinkle, twinkle little star'. Sometimes, though, when she messes up my stuff, she gets on my nerves a bit."

### Israel

Tali has family in Israel. "I went there once when I was two, but I don't remember much about it. But I think I remember a place full of pomegranate trees with enormous pomegranates, and I've seen our photos of lovely waterfalls in the middle of the desert, where King David is supposed to have hidden from Saul. I'd love to go again one day."

### Singing and sewing and sports

Learning Welsh was easy, Tali says. "I picked it up from my friends, and now I really like the Eisteddfod, and enjoy taking part in the singing and craft competitions. Our school choir won a prize at the Cardiff Urdd Eisteddfod and I also won first prize and a trophy for textiles. I love sewing and have my own sewing machine – it was my grandma's. I designed a quilt for baby Jacob and I am making a hobby-horse for Isabelle's birthday.

I have plenty of time for my hobbies because we don't have a TV, but we do watch videos. I'm quite sporty, too, and have won prizes for the high jump and relay. In netball, I play goalkeeper because I'm quite tall."

## Books

Tali loves reading and it's not surprising that she especially likes books about horses, like *How to take care of your pony* and pony stories as well. "I read them in Welsh too, and I have a copy of *Shani'r Shetland*. I'm also inspired by Christian books like *The Watchmaker's Daughter* and *The Children's Champion*. I always have a lot of books on the go at the same time, usually because I lose one when I'm half through!"

## Tali's likes and dislikes about food

"I've been a vegetarian since the age of six. I came back from school one day and said I wasn't going to eat meat any more. I just couldn't stop thinking of the poor animals that had been killed. When the rest of the family eat turkey for Christmas dinner, I just have something special like a nut roast.

My favourite food is pizza. I also like chocolate and 'matza brai' – Jewish food where you crush bits of unleavened bread, mix them with egg and fry them with cinnamon, stewed apple and sugar. It's a real treat for breakfast."

## Precious things

"My favourite thing is my Bible, and Miss Bunny, a big toy rabbit which used to be bigger than me," says Tali. "I had it when I had an operation when I was a baby. And I love Skipper, a toy dog which my mum gave me when we moved here."

## Pets, birds and bears

Tali and her family have a dog and three cats, and a garden with a lot of birds. She also likes bears. "If you look at a bear enjoying itself, its body is magnificent, and so huge. The cubs are cute too. I loved the film called *The Bear*, though it was really sad."

## Helping with housework

Tali doesn't mind hoovering and ironing. She likes cooking, too, and says she can make a good Celtic soup, which is a bit like *cawl*. She makes cakes too. "But I'm a bit lazy sometimes. My bedroom's usually a bit of a tip."

## And when she grows up

Tali used to want to be a pilot or a flying vet. "I went to an air show and it got me excited about flying. But I've gone off the idea now because I don't fancy crashing. I really have no idea any more what I want to be!"

# Adam

| age | 11 |
|-----|-----|
| birthday | January |
| home | the sea-side town of Barry in the Vale of Glamorgan |
| family | his parents and sister, 12 and brother, 5 |

*"Cardiff Devils' ice-hockey centre is my second home, and my idea of heaven would be an enormous ice-hockey rink!"*

### Hockey–yee-essss!

Adam is mad about ice-hockey. He plays for Cardiff Devils' under-14 and under-16 teams, and practises seven days a week – well, nearly. "One night, just for a change, I go ice-skating. But other nights, it's ice-hockey. And then maybe there'll be a game on the Saturday or Sunday, and every fortnight I play somewhere in England. I'm used to going away from home. I've been three times to the Netherlands, and once to Germany."

Recently, Adam won a prize for the best centre player in a tournament in Hull. The prize was an 'All Stars' tee-shirt, which is now safely in his bedroom along with 75 medals and other trophies.

"I was really surprised, because I didn't think I'd played all that well," he says. "I was glad I had, though. Things like that are important for me, because I'm a very competitive person."

### How he started playing

Adam began by playing street or roller-hockey out in the road with a gang of older boys, when he was about six. He used to play with a tennis-racquet, and the other boys said he couldn't play with them any more unless he had a proper hockey-stick. He went home and told his mum. "In the end, I got the hockey-stick, and I started playing, and before long I went to play for this local team.

Then, Dad saw an advertisement in the paper about ice-hockey. I went for trials with the Cardiff Devils, and I was selected. I was seven. The family decided they wanted to see a game, and that was it, then, Mum says. We were all hooked! My little brother's gone bananas on the game, too, and the two of us practise in the garden and on the wooden floor in our lounge – it's excellent! – or on Barry beach. Dannielle used to play as well, but now she plays field hockey for the school."

## A pricey game

This is the kit Adam needs to play ice-hockey:

helmet, shoulder-pads, elbow- and knee-pads, gloves, shirt, a box to protect sensitive parts, shorts and braces, protection net, socks and suspenders to cover shin-pads, and skating boots.

### Total cost of the kit

| | |
|---|---|
| whole kit | £600 |
| *(a new one is needed every two years)* | |
| boots | over £100 |
| hockey-stick | over £100 |
| training | £52 a month |
| every away game | £25 |

"I'm lucky that Mum and Dad are so supportive," says Adam. "Dad works twelve hours a day for British Telecom to pay for things and Mum helps in Gran's bread shop. In the summer, I'll be off to a hockey camp in Toronto, Ontario, and I'm already saving up money in an empty water-bottle. A big one!"

## Training

Cardiff Devils train talented young people to become professional players. Adam's dream is to be able to go to a specialist sports college in Canada at the end of Year 7. There, he would have to practise every morning before lessons. "You have to have a good education before you can play ice-hockey," he says. "I'll be staying on in school till I'm old enough to go to college, because the NHL (National Hockey League) select players for the League from the best college students. And I want to get a good education, so that I can get a good job and earn good money."

## Adam 'Jekyll and Hyde'?

Adam claims that he's usually a very gentle boy. "Honest! But on the field, I seem to change into someone else." This 'other Adam' can sometimes get into trouble. "I've had too many penalty minutes this year. If you do something you shouldn't, you have to go into this box."

Fortunately, though, he's able to leave his bad feelings behind on the field. At home, Adam's good at helping. He does the washing-up – sometimes without being asked – and sometimes, the cleaning as well. He's fond of his little brother, and takes Rhys to the fair or the beach to play. And in school, where they are taught in Welsh, Adam always keeps an eye on Rhys. "He'll come to me if he thinks somebody's been nasty to him. 'Give them a hiding, Adam,' he'll say. But I say, 'No. Go and tell a teacher'." Adam dosen't like violence, or guns on the street, and he wishes there was a world where people weren't killed.

Though Adam isn't able to change everything, hopefully one day he will achieve his goal of becoming a professional ice-hockey player.

# Lleucu

| | |
|---|---|
| **age** | 10 |
| **birthday** | March |
| **home** | Carmarthen |
| **family** | mother and twin sisters, 7 |
| **interests** | folk- and clog-dancing, netball, the Urdd youth club, shopping and socialising |

*Lleucu*

> "*My name means 'sunbeam', and I'm a happy person. If people are nasty to my friends, I always go up to them and say, 'Stop that'. My idea of heaven is a place where no one quarrels.*"

## Family and friends

Lleucu lives in Carmarthen with her mother and twin sisters, Erin and Ffion. Her father lives in London. She hasn't always lived in Carmarthen – she was born in a place called Caerphilly, but the family moved when she was a year old. She gets on well with the twins, though she says they get on her nerves at times. "When I'm trying to do my homework, they keep coming in. They're so noisy!"

How would Lleucu's friends describe her? "As a lively person who likes work and who'd do anything good they asked me to do," she says. On her tenth birthday, she had a sleepover.

"We talk and go to bed late and get up early, and eat sweets and crisps. Sometimes, we play games like Monopoly, but we didn't play a lot of games this year, just talked and had a laugh. We went to sleep about 2 am, and got up at 6.30. I had a mobile phone for a birthday present. I like sending messages to my friends, and playing games. But we're not allowed to take them to school."

## Mam's illness

Three years ago, Lleucu's mother became ill with brain cancer. Lleucu had to help her Dad-cu and Mam-gu look after the twins. Her mother had to have surgery and chemotherapy to remove the growth. The family has just had good news – the cancer has all gone.

"Mam getting better is the best thing that's ever happened to me," says Lleucu. "She became ill when I was seven. I remember her going into hospital. I didn't know what was happening at the time. Mam-gu and Dad-cu said she was ill, and that was about it. The twins knew Mam was ill, and, well, they wanted a cwtsh sometimes, because they knew Mam wasn't here. We put a poster up in the window when she came home. It said, 'Welcome home, Mam'. I was so happy when I heard she was better. I gave her a big hug!"

Lleucu's mother works as a waitress now in one of the cafés in town. She has raised money to buy a new machine for Singleton Hospital. She organised a sponsored walk, two concerts and a barbecue. "I'm saving up now, too – we're all going to Florida next year to swim with the dolphins. I've already got £20 and I'd like to have £50 altogether."

## The dancing girl

Dancing is in Lleucu's blood – folk dancing and clog dancing. She dances,  her mother used to dance when she was young, and Mam-gu and Dad-cu are still dancing! Lleucu belongs to a group called Hafod Wennog. She has to wear special shoes called clogs, like the ones people used to wear in Holland. She learns special dance steps, too – walking and skipping, the heel step and 'pitter-patter'. Her favourite dance is 'Llanthony Abbey', because of its tune and the dance steps.

"Clog-dancing is quite easy when you know what you're doing," says Lleucu. "I don't want to be in a group when I grow up, though, because I'd rather stay close to Mam."

## School

Lleucu is in Year Five. She didn't speak English at all before she went to nursery school. "Everybody should learn Welsh. It's the best language of all!"

Her school encourages sports. Lleucu is looking forward to next year, when she will have a chance to be in the school netball team. She already plays centre and goalie for the town's team. "I'd like to be an air hostess or lawyer when I grow up, the first because I like going on holiday, and a lawyer because I think it would be a good job to have."

## At the weekend

Every Friday, Lleucu goes to the local branch of Urdd Gobaith Cymru, a youth club. They rehearse for the Urdd Eisteddfod as well as playing sports and games. On Saturdays, she likes going to town to shop in places like Tammy Girl, and on Sundays she goes to Sunday School. Her grandmother teaches some of the younger children there. Sometimes she goes to the beach at Llansteffan on a Sunday, to collect shells or walk up to the castle.

Until about three years ago, Lleucu had an alsatian called Stella. "I felt very sad when she died. I cried and cried. I'd like another dog – a labrador this time," she says.

She likes reading, too – books by Enid Blyton, Roald Dahl and T. Llew Jones. "My favourite story is *You Can't Please Everybody*, by Enid Blyton. I agree – you really can't please everybody all of the time!"

## Did you know?

● In 1405, 5000 Frenchmen from Brittany landed at Milford Haven in Pembrokeshire. They marched to Carmarthen, and with the help of Owain Glyndŵr and his army, they took the castle from the English. Owain wanted the Welsh people to have the right to rule themselves, and to have their own university. At this time, he led many bloody attacks on the walled towns and castles of Wales to try to take them over. He was crowned Prince of Wales and held the first Welsh parliament at Machynlleth, but in the end he was defeated, and disappeared. No one knows what really happened to him.

● Nearly 400 years later, the French landed again, this time in Fishguard. However, they were defeated by an army of Welsh women, led by a tall, stout and determined woman called Jemima Nicholas.

● In 1843, Rebecca's Daughters raised a great riot in Carmarthen. They were really men dressed as women who were protesting against the high taxes they had to pay to travel on the roads. With their faces blackened, they charged into the town on horseback, and attacked the workhouse until mounted soldiers called 'Dragoons' came and drove them away.

● Trouble with your homework? Maybe the new BBC website – https://jam.bbc.co.uk can help you with some subjects! Why not have a look?

# Michael

> *"In school, I feel Welsh, especially when we celebrate St. David's Day and talk about things that happened in Wales, but outside school, I feel more English. Mum comes from Gloucestershire, even though she's lived here nearly all her life, and her dad's from London. And my Nan lives just across the town bridge on the English side of the river Wye but she has a free bus pass so she can nip over to see us any time."*

| | |
|---|---|
| **age** | 10 |
| **birthday** | June |
| **home** | a housing estate near Chepstow in Monmouthshire |
| **family** | parents and sister, 13 |
| **interests** | fixing cars, cricket, Scouts, reading and Big Band music |

## Michael's family

Michael lives on the Welsh side of the river Severn. A generation ago, his father's family used to speak Welsh. They moved to the area from Cheshire in the 1970s to work in the building trade. At that time, lots of houses were being built in that part of Monmouthshire, because new homes were needed after the Severn bridge and the M4 motorway made it easier for people to travel between England and Wales. His mum and dad met at a local dance, and used to play darts together too. "Mum says I'm Celtic, because I have Scottish blood as well as Welsh and English, and I'm named after St. Michael's Mount in Cornwall. My sister's name is Cornish, too."

Michael's father is a carpenter, and his mother works in local government. She's also a parent-governor in Michael's school. Kerensa goes to the local comprehensive school, and she helps Michael to revise his mental mathematics. "Usually, we get on well, but not always," Michael says.

The whole family enjoys music. "Kerensa plays the flute. I learn the clarinet in school, and I love listening to Glen Miller and Big Band dance music. I pretend I'm conducting. My grandad gave me a tape of Kenny Rogers and that started me off. And once, with the Greater Gwent Massed Choir, I sang 'The Lion King' in the Royal Albert Hall in London."

## Grandad

Michael's grandad trained as a mechanic and he and Michael are mad about cars. "He can fix anything," Michael says. "He had a Ford Sierra for about fifteen years, and a Ford Fiesta which cost £20 but didn't last long. The clutch burnt out. There was a Fiat Uno, too, whose pistons didn't work very well. He explains all the parts, he's like, 'Oh that's the carburettor,' or whatever. He can't walk very well now and I get bread and milk for him every day and Mum makes roast dinners for him and Grandma."

## Family outings

Sometimes the family goes shopping to Newport or Cwmbran to the scouts shop to get his uniform. Michael says he is "not fussed about clothes"; he likes casual t-shirts and jogging bottoms, and especially the latest Man United shirts. He has some which date back to the 1980s. In Newport, he and his dad often go to the cinema to see films like Harry Potter. They've also taken the ferry across the Usk under Newport's famous transporter bridge.

Michael says: "It's scary going across because the bridge above is hanging on wires and Dad says things like 'Look out – it's going to snap in a minute!'

And sometimes we go cycling across the old Severn bridge, or go for walks by the estuary. There used to be ferries near Beachley on our side to take people over to Aust on the English side. The boats were called the *Severn King*, the *Severn Queen* and the *Severn Princess*. But they're not needed any more because of the two Severn bridges."

## School

Michael likes the idea of learning and doing well, and would like to be a teacher when he grows up, though he says: "Children don't really know till later what they want to be. Our headmistress has a display of our work over two stages called 'Reach for the Stars' to show us how our work can get better if we work hard. My handwriting's in it, and I can see how it's improved over the year." He likes reading, writing stories and poems, and wrote a poem about fish for a poetry competition. "I've read Harry Potter (J.K. Rowling used to live round here), Michael Morpurgo – *The Sleeping Sword*, about King Arthur – and Mum's old Enid Blyton books."

## If Michael won £100,000

…as well as giving some to his grandparents, he thinks he'd put some aside "to pay for my and Kerensa's university fees, and some to Cancer Research, OXFAM, the NSPCC and the RSPCA. I wouldn't keep it all myself."

## And what he'd really, really like to see happening in the world would be

- for everyone to be reasonably well-off ("not rich, or they'd all be selfish")
- for everyone to have the same chance to 'reach for the stars' and go to university and achieve their potential
- for everyone to be treated the same, whatever their job, race or language. Michael's mum says: "We're all different colours of the same rainbow."

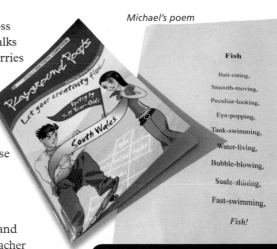

*Michael's poem*

**Fish**

Bait-eating,
Smooth-moving,
Peculiar-looking,
Eye-popping,
Tank-swimming,
Water-living,
Bubble-blowing,
Scale-shining,
Fast-swimming,

Fish!

## Did you know?

- that the clay mudflats around the Severn estuary have preserved all kinds of strange artefacts from the past, like the three sets of prehistoric footprints, two male and one child found not far from Uskmouth Power Station? The owners might have been searching for their next meal, because not far away from them was a tool called a mattock, made from a red deer antler, which could have been used to uncover cockles. And when Newport's Arts Centre was being excavated, a medieval ship was found buried on the shore of the river Usk. Tree-ring dating showed that its timber came from an oak tree felled between September 1465 and April 1466. It was possibly a Portuguese ship, captured and brought there by pirates.

- that if you want to be an engineer or an environmental scientist, you can see in Michael's home area four magnificent examples of what engineers and scientists can build by working together? First, there's the Severn Railway Tunnel, the longest main-line railway tunnel in the UK. It took thirteen years to build and opened for the first goods train in 1886. Then there's Newport's Transporter Bridge, designed by a French engineer called Ferdinand Arnodin and completed in 1906. It was high enough to allow high-masted sailing ships to pass underneath it as well as enabling people and horses to cross the river Usk. And there are the two great Severn bridges. One opened in 1966 and the other in 1996. All these have helped to attract more business and jobs into south-east Wales by making it easier for people and goods to travel.

# Lowri

*"I like climbing trees and mountains. Yes, I am a tomboy, but I do like 'girly' things as well, like trendy clothes and painting my nails. My big sister Hana's the one to blame for this – she's a fashionaholic!"*

| | |
|---|---|
| **age** | 10 |
| **birthday** | March |
| **home** | near Dolgellau, Gwynedd |
| **family** | parents and 1 sister, 2 brothers |
| **interests** | climbing and running, acting, karate, reading, mathematics and fashion |

## Lowri's family

Lowri lives in the countryside at the foot of Cader Idris with her parents, sister Hana, brothers Ioan and Cai, two cats called Mabon and Mabli, a kitten called Modlen, one hamster and a dog called Moss.

"Mabon and Mabli are really old for cats – 14 years old – older than me! Moss once bit a friend of my mother's on the leg. Cai has a ferret called Mêl, because its fur smells a bit like honey, which is *mêl* in Welsh. We had two Vietnamese pot-bellied pigs for years. I wouldn't mind being a vet when I grow up, though I'd rather be an actress."

Lowri's mother works for the local council and shoots clay pigeons in her spare time. She's a good shot, Lowri says. Her father teaches Art and PE and is a very good photographer and artist, too. "He used to design the posters for the Sesiwn Fawr music festival. Here's some of his work…

Hana's 17 and she likes wearing make-up and going out. Ioan's 15 and he's into trial bikes and playing rugby. Cai, who's 13, likes climbing mountains and shooting – and playing with Mêl the ferret.

It's good being the youngest in the family because I get all the attention. I do sometimes act the baby, but because I spend so much time with older children, I can be quite mature too. The only thing I don't like about being the youngest is that the others boss me around, especially Cai."

## Lowri enjoys

✔ **karate** "I do it for self-defence and to keep fit, though I'm not allowed to practise at home in case I break Mam's ornaments. I've got an orange belt at the moment. I hope to get a black belt by my thirteenth birthday."

✔ **mathematics** (problem-solving especially)

✔ **playing fast tunes on the fiddle** which is purple!

✔ **acting** "I really, really love acting. I'm best at comic parts. I can't do sad parts because I have fits of giggles. Once I acted one of the ugly sisters in a school play and that was a fantastic experience. And I acted an old woman in the chapel play, but I spoke much too quickly. My favourite actress is the one who acts Buffy – Sarah Michelle Gellar – but I'm a fan of Catherine Zeta Jones too."

## Going to Sunday School

Lowri says that nobody makes her go, she just goes because she enjoys it. "I give out hymns in chapel – from the pulpit! We're not a religious family, like saying our prayers before going to bed and so on, but I do believe in Jesus Christ. I'm the only member of the family who goes to Sunday School. We sing and listen to stories for the first twenty minutes, then we go to the vestry to have lessons about the Bible, and make models and things. It's great."

## Books and writing

"I'm mad about Harry Potter books, and I like reading Pippy Longstocking stories in Welsh, too, as well as writing my own stories, especially fantasies about witches and magic. I try to write in my diary every day, though I don't always remember. Nobody's allowed to look at it, because I write stuff about people in it!"

## Running Competitions

Every year, Lowri runs the Llyn Tegid Race, the Cader Idris Race, the RSPB Race in Penmaen-pŵl and Race The Train in Abergynolwyn. "They're all between one and five miles long, so I do a bit of training for them. I run with people in their seventies! I never win, but it's really brill. The important thing is to take part, isn't it?"

## Lowri's collections

"I've got masses of things like Beanie Babies in my bedroom, but my favourite is Pol Pot, a little bronze piglet. He reminds me of the pigs we used to have. Mam didn't want to buy him for me, but I said I would treasure him. And I always have done."

## What she doesn't like

"I can't stand mushy peas. A plateful would be my idea of hell. And I don't like having to make difficult decisions. I never want to let anyone down, and I try all the time to keep everybody happy. That's what I'm looking forward to when I'll be grown up: being able to make decisions. Oh, and being able to drive, of course – either a Land Rover or a Mini Cooper."

## Lowri's idea of heaven

"…would be some-where pink and fluffy where I could eat (pink!) candyfloss all day and play Monopoly with Tchaikovsky's 'Sugar Plum Fairy' as back-ground music. And I'd know everybody there."

## A new portrait!

# Name _____

Stick a photograph (or a drawing) here

age _____
birthday _____
home _____
_____
_____
family _____
_____
_____
interests _____
_____
_____

"
_____
_____
_____
_____
_____
"

signature

Stick a photograph here... e.g. of a pet, house or the locality

**Family, pets and home**

Stick a photograph here... perhaps of other family members

**And how about school?**

Stick a photograph here to do with school or hobbies

If you want to print off a copy of these two pages, go to the website www.gomer.co.uk – look in Teachers' Resources!

Stick a photograph here to do with school or hobbies

**Interests / friends**

Stick a photograph here... perhaps to go with the 'Did you know?' box

**Did you know?**

• _____

_____

_____

_____

_____

_____

_____

• _____

_____

_____

_____

_____

_____

_____

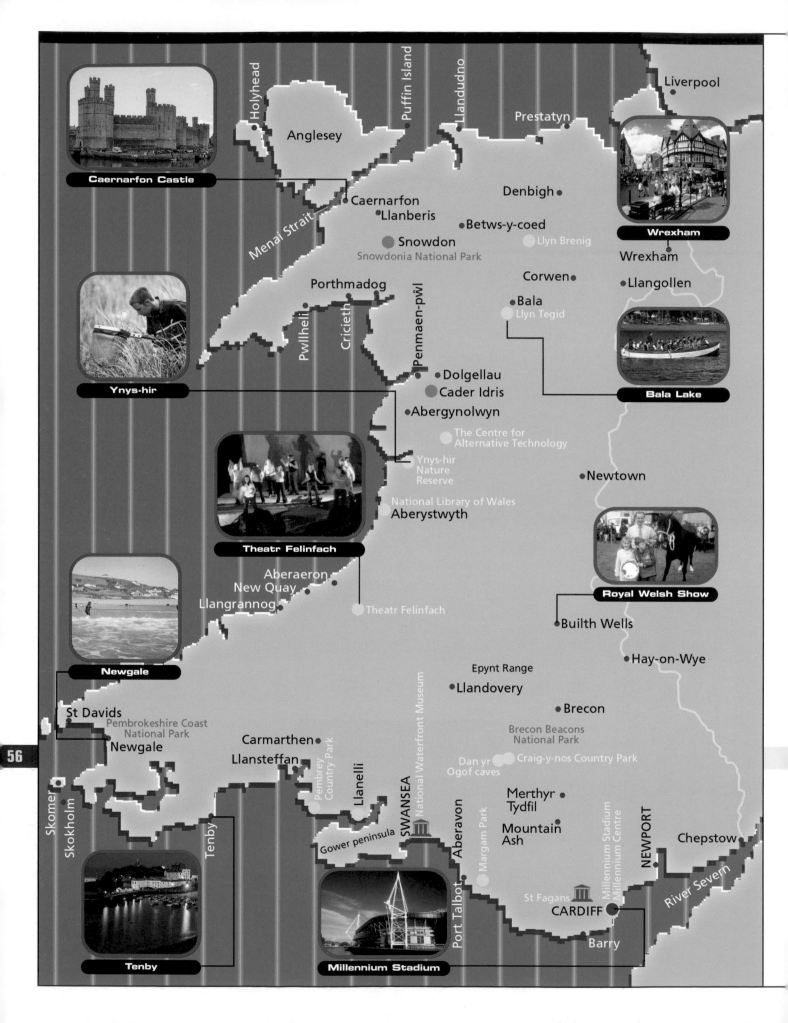

Caernarfon Castle

Ynys-hir

Newgale

Tenby

Wrexham

Bala Lake

Royal Welsh Show

Theatr Felinfach

Millennium Stadium

Holyhead
Anglesey
Puffin Island
Llandudno
Liverpool
Prestatyn
Denbigh
Caernarfon
Llanberis
Betws-y-coed
Snowdon
Llyn Brenig
Snowdonia National Park
Wrexham
Corwen
Llangollen
Porthmadog
Penmaen-pŵl
Bala
Llyn Tegid
Pwllheli
Cricieth
Dolgellau
Cader Idris
Abergynolwyn
The Centre for Alternative Technology
Ynys-hir Nature Reserve
Newtown
National Library of Wales
Aberystwyth
Aberaeron
New Quay
Llangrannog
Theatr Felinfach
Builth Wells
Hay-on-Wye
Epynt Range
Llandovery
Brecon
St Davids
Pembrokeshire Coast National Park
Newgale
Carmarthen
Llansteffan
Brecon Beacons National Park
Dan yr Ogof caves
Craig-y-nos Country Park
Skomer
Skokholm
Pembrey Country Park
Llanelli
SWANSEA
National Waterfront Museum
Merthyr Tydfil
Mountain Ash
Tenby
Gower peninsula
Aberavon
Margam Park
Port Talbot
Millennium Stadium
Millennium Centre
NEWPORT
Chepstow
St Fagans
CARDIFF
River Severn
Barry

## St Fagans

Want to be a Celtic warrior with a painted face to scare off your enemies and keep away evil spirits, and wear clothes made from wool and leather? You could warm yourself by the wood fire in the middle of the floor in the round house, and choke in the smoke. Hmm.

St Fagans

Perhaps you'd prefer to try your hand at throwing a pot in the pottery. Or what about dressing up like a pupil in the age of Victoria, sitting behind a desk and squirming under the beady eyes of the threatening teacher? It may be you who will have to wear the 'Welsh Not' placard around your neck because someone heard you speak in Welsh. Why not go for a walk, instead? There might be a sty full of piglets, or spring lambs in the fields as you wander around the houses and gardens. Take your torch if you go to the Hallowe'en Festival. In December, you could join in traditional Christmas activities, sing carols and have a mince pie. Where could you sample these weird and wonderful things? In the National History Museum, St Fagans, near Cardiff.

## The Centre for Alternative Technology

Do you and your family recycle every piece of paper, every tin and every bottle? Do you have a compost heap of potato peel and banana skins to make fertiliser which helps the garden grow? Do you always switch off the lights when not in use? And use long-life light bulbs? Well, if you do, you're an excellent recycler, and very aware of environmental issues. You'd love the Centre for Alternative Technology at Machynlleth. The Centre's purpose is to show us how to live without wasting resources or spoiling the world around us. Go there, and you can ride on a mountain railway powered by water. In the Wind Pavilion and the Power House, you can try out ways of using the power of wind, rain, sun and tide to create energy. Want a go as a bus driver? Sit in the driver's seat and pretend to drive. See for yourself how carbon dioxide pollutes the air.

The Centre for Alternative Technology

## Snowdon

You *could* walk to the top of Wales's highest mountain, but it would be a long and challenging journey. It's much easier to take the Snowdon Mountain Railway from the village of Llanberis. To the peak, 1085 metres above sea level, it's a five-mile journey. When you get there, you (and, during the summer, thousands of others) can enjoy the fantastic view: the Irish mountains, the islands of Anglesey and Man and the coast of northern England. Nearer, you are surrounded by mile upon mile of the majestic mountains, valleys and lakes of the Snowdonia National Park. *Eryri*, the

Snowdon

Welsh word for Snowdonia, means 'the land where the eagle lives'. The village of Llanberis was once famous for its slate quarries, where three thousand men worked. In the Slate Museum in the village, you can discover just how hard life was for the quarrymen – and you might learn how to split a slate as well.

## The National Urdd Eisteddfod

This is the largest competitive youth festival in Europe. It is held in alternate years in different places in north and south Wales, and every four years it is held in the Millennium Centre in Cardiff, where the Urdd has its home. Thousands of children and young people take part in all kinds of competitions, from sports and athletics, disco- and folk-dancing to art, crafts, science, literature, singing (pop, folk, and classical), instrumental music and so on. Rhys Ifans, Ioan Gruffydd, Bryn Terfel, Tara Bethan and Nia Roberts have all been competitors in the past and they all agree that performing on the Urdd Eisteddfod stage was an inspiration.

The National Urdd Eisteddfod

Lapland

Germany

Corfu

Europe

Asia

Greece

Nepal

Africa

Iraq

Israel

Australasia

Brisbane

Sudan

Cape of Good Hope

59

There are more recipes from the children of Wales on the website www.gomer.co.uk – look in Teachers' Resources!

## Chocolate cornflake cakes

You need:

150g (6oz) cooking chocolate

75g (3oz) cornflakes

1 adult to help perhaps

Melt the chocolate in a small bowl set over a large bowl of very hot, freshly boiled, water. Very carefully pour the melted chocolate over the cornflakes and mix thoroughly. With a spoon, share the mixture between 12 paper cases. Put them in the fridge to harden.

A special thank you to Rhys for giving us a complete recipe for chocolate cornflake cakes – this is a great one for any young cook to try.

"I like making spicy food like curry and chilli. Or I'll make a cake, or an apple tart."
Gruffudd

"I like making chocolate cornflake cakes."
Rhys

"If I bake, I like to make a plain sponge."
Simeon

"I love every kind of seafood, especially mussels."
Luke

"I love tea, and I take a cuppa to my bedroom!"
Arfon

"Some of my favourite puddings are apple crumble, apple tart and spotted dick. And Turkish Delight."
Robert

## Thank you

*Greetings from the authors who interviewed the children*

**Meleri Wyn James**

❝*Life would be very boring if we were all exactly the same – being a bit different can be a very good thing! I hope you will enjoy reading about all the different children in this book.* ❞

**Bethan Gwanas**

❝*Thank to the bunch who let me ask them all those silly questions, and thanks to you for reading the results. Enjoy – I did!* ❞

**Gwion Hallam**

❝*When is work never work? When you're writing for Welsh children, in a book for Welsh children and in the words of the Welsh children themselves. One country but a nation of children. To the children I met: thank you for showing us your Wales, and ours.* ❞

**Elin Meek**

❝*Thank you for the lovely welcome and for your enthusiasm in answering my questions. You made my work really easy!* ❞

**Eileen Jones**

❝*Thank you for sharing your interesting lives with me to prepare this book. It was wonderful to meet you and your families and to learn about your experiences and hopes for the future.* ❞

**Ann Saer**

❝*Kids, you were brilliant. A million thanks to you and your families for letting me in to your busy lives and being so open and chatty. I hope you'lll enjoy getting to know each other and the different parts of Wales where you live as much as I have!* ❞

# Index

## Acknowledgements

I should like to thank most warmly all those who contributed to the project which led to this publication: the network of individuals who introduced us to the children portrayed; the team of authors, photographers and designer – Olwen Fowler; NSPCC Cymru for their advice and direction; members of the Monitoring Group; Pont Books, Gomer Press for drawing all the threads together; and above all, the children and their families for their enthusiasm, their warm welcome and ready co-operation.

*Ann Saer*

The publishers gratefully acknowledge the excellent work of the following photographers:
David Barnes
Martin Caveney
Aled Hughes
Gerallt Llywelyn
For permission to reproduce other photographs, thanks also to: Andy Hay and rspb-images.com; Theatr Felinfach; Gwersyll yr Urdd, Glan-llyn; Wrexham County Borough Council; (all for pictures on p.56) and for pictures on p. 57: The National History Museum, St Fagans; The Centre for Alternative Technology; Lluniau Llwyfan.